Contents

Introduction

World Class Readings 2 is an intermediate level text for nonnative speakers of English. It is part of the *World Class Readings* series. The primary focus of this series is reading, but there are also exercises to improve students' skills in listening, speaking, and writing. The readings are appropriate both for students learning English for strictly academic purposes and for those learning English for more general reasons.

World Class Readings practices and develops many of the skills that are needed to do well on standardized English tests, such as TOEFL®, TOEIC®, and IELTS®. Using this series, therefore, is a good way for a student to prepare for those important exams.

Organization of the Book

World Class Readings 2 consists of fourteen units centered around a reading. Each unit has the following components:

1. Warm-Up Questions

This section serves to draw students into the reading in a number of ways. The questions prompt students to skim the text and use the pictures that open the unit to make predictions about the reading. They encourage students to share information they may already have about the topic and solicit students' opinions on issues that are raised in the reading.

2. Vocabulary Preview

This section consists of short segments taken directly from the reading. A word or a phrase in each segment is highlighted . These items are vocabulary terms that are important to an overall understanding of the reading.

3. While You Read

This exercise supplies a list of important topics that are discussed in the reading, presented out of order. Students need to number these topics in the order in which they appear in the reading. The exercise helps students understand the structure of the reading and provides practice in skimming for important points.

4. The Reading

The reading, ranging in length from about 600 to 850 words, is the heart of each unit. Cultural and topic-specific vocabulary and concepts that might be unfamiliar to readers are footnoted.

5. Understanding the Reading

This section, consisting of eight multiple-choice questions, builds students' comprehension of the reading. Most of these are explicit detail questions that can be answered by skimming the reading, but some require students to draw inferences from the reading. This part of the unit is closest to the reading section of a number of standardized exams, including TOEFL® and TOEIC®.

6. Vocabulary Building

This exercise consists of vocabulary taken from the reading and eight sentences unrelated to the reading. Each sentence has a blank that students fill in with a word from the vocabulary list. Students use the context of the sentence to make the choice.

7. Reading Skill

This part of the unit focuses on individual reading skills and features an exercise that allows students to apply that skill to the reading. A comprehensive list of these skills appears on page 182.

8. Focus on Listening

The audio program for World Class Readings contains statements about the reading passages. Students listen to these statements and answer true or false questions about the reading. This activity provides listening practice and helps prepare students for certain listening activities in standardized tests.

9. Writing and Discussion Questions

This section consists of topics related to the theme of the reading. In most units, at least one of these items asks students who have Internet access to use the web as a research tool and as a source of further reading material on the same theme.

10. Crossword Puzzle

Each unit ends with a crossword puzzle. The words used to solve the puzzle come from the Vocabulary Preview and Vocabulary Building exercises and from topic-specific vocabulary in the reading. It serves as a review of vocabulary introduced in the unit.

The *Teacher's Manual*

The Teacher's Manual contains quizzes, one for each unit, which can be photocopied and given to students as a graded test or as a final review of the unit. The Teacher's Manual also has a complete answer key, as well as an audio script for the listening activity.

I hope that the students and teachers who use this book will find it enjoyable. The English language skills and the information in the readings are meant to be fun, as well as useful. I hope that they provide glimpses into that huge, diverse, and interdependent culture, not of one country, but of the world.

Bruce Rogers

The author and the publisher would like to thank all the people whose comments, reviews, and assistance were invaluable in the development of *World Class Readings*.

It's a New World Record!

Fig. 1.1

Before You Read

» Warm-Up Questions

Discuss these questions in pairs or groups. Share your ideas with the class.

1. What do you think is happening in the photograph above?

2. Look at the title of the unit. What is a world record?

3. Have you ever hear of the *Guiness World Records* book? What do you know about it?

❱ Vocabulary Preview

These statements come from the reading "It's a New World Record!" Read each statement and then answer the questions that follow. Check your answers before you begin the reading.

The name Sir Hugh Beaver may not mean much to most people, but his brainchild —*Guinness World Records*—is known around the world.

1. Sir Hugh's *brainchild* is . . .

    (A) his intelligent young child.
    (B) an imaginary son or daughter.
    (C) his creation.

Sir Hugh had a brilliant idea.

2. A *brilliant* idea is . . .

    (A) a smart idea.
    (B) an idea that he worked on with others.
    (C) a shocking idea.

He decided that a thorough, reliable guide to records was needed.

3. A guide that is *thorough* and *reliable* is . . .

    (A) long and boring.
    (B) complete and dependable.
    (C) new and improved.

They opened a Guinness Records office in London, and, after a year of hard work, the first slim volume was published.

4. A *slim* volume is . . . book.

    (A) an attractive
    (B) a short
    (C) a valuable

Some people use the book to settle arguments about scientific facts; others use it to resolve debates about sports.

5. Circle another phrase in this sentence that has the same meaning as *resolve debates*.

The Taiwan museum is unique .

6. A museum that is *unique* is . . .

    (A) historic.
    (B) unlike any others.
    (C) full of interesting collections.

Most people, though, enjoy looking through the book for wacky world records.

7. If a record is *wacky*, it is . . .

    (A) crazy and funny.
    (B) difficult to break.
    (C) completely unbelievable.

Then there was David Kremmer from Wisconsin, U.S.A., who stacked ten bowling balls on top of each other, or John Evans of the U.K., who balanced a car on his head for thirty-three seconds.

8. The word *stacked* means . . .

    (A) rolled.
    (B) put one on top of another.
    (C) threw into the air.

Its main hall resembles an enormous *Guinness World Records* book, and its snack bar looks like a giant hamburger.

9. Find and circle another word that means *enormous*.

Or you could break the record for getting into a bathtub with the most live, venomous snakes.

10. Venomous snakes are . . .

    (A) poisonous.
    (B) quite large.
    (C) ones that live in water.

While You Read

Here are seven points that appear in the reading passage. There is one point for each paragraph. While you read, put the points in order from 1 to 7.

_____ Types of records listed in the book
_____ Sir Hugh's idea for a record book
_____ Some records you can try to break
_____ Sir Hugh's argument with his friends
_____ What happens when you break a record
_____ Guinness records on television, on the Internet, and in museums
_____ The birth and success of *Guinness World Records*

IT'S A NEW WORLD RECORD!

1   The name Sir Hugh Beaver may not mean much to most people, but his brainchild—*Guinness World Records*—is known around the world. Here is how it all started: Sir Hugh was the managing director of the Guinness Brewery.[1] One day in 1951, Sir Hugh was hunting with some friends in southeastern Ireland. He shot at a kind of bird called the golden plover, but he missed. Sir Hugh said that, in his opinion, the golden plover was the fastest flying game bird[2] in all of Europe. Some of the people in his party disagreed. They said that the fastest game bird was another type of bird, the grouse. Sir Hugh decided to check the facts. He and his friends searched through many reference books in a library, but none of them had much information about the fastest, the biggest, the most expensive, or the oldest.

2   Sir Hugh had a brilliant idea. He realized that, every day, there are hundreds of arguments similar to the one that he had had with his friends. He also realized that many of these arguments took place in pubs[3] and bars where his company's products were sold. He decided that a thorough, reliable guide to records was needed.

Of course, he liked the idea that this guide would indirectly
promote Guinness products.   20

3   Several years later, in September 1954, Sir Hugh approached
Norris and Ross McWhirter. These twin brothers operated a fact-
finding agency. Sir Hugh asked them to collect and publish a
guide to records in as many fields as possible. The McWhirter
brothers opened a Guinness Records office in London, and, after   25
a year of hard work, the first slim volume was published in the
U.K. By the end of the year, the book climbed to the top of the
British best-seller list.[4] In 1956, the Guinness company published
the record book in the United States. It was also an instant success
there. Updated every year, *Guinness World Records* has sold more   30
than ninety million copies in seventy-seven different countries
and in thirty-seven languages. In fact, the book holds a record of
its own: it has sold more copies than any other book except the
Bible and the Koran.[5]

4   *Guinness World Records* has been called the world's most   35
readable reference book. The records are divided into thirteen
categories. Some people use the book to settle arguments about
scientific facts; others use it to resolve debates about sports. Most
people, though, enjoy looking through the book for wacky world
records. One of the most unusual is the record set by Christian   40
Adam of Germany. Adam rode his bicycle 60.45 kilometers while
playing the violin. Oh, and by the way, he rode *backwards* when
he set this record! Then there was David Kremmer from
Wisconsin, U.S.A., who stacked ten bowling balls on top of each
other, or John Evans of the U.K., who balanced a car on his head   45
for thirty-three seconds.

5   For those who cannot get enough information about records
from the book, there are Guinness World Records Museums

Fig. 1.2 The Taiwan Guinness World Records Museum.
Top Main hall.
Bottom Snack bar.

located throughout North America and Europe, and one recently opened in Taiwan. The Taiwan museum is unique. Its main hall resembles an enormous *Guinness World Records* book, and its snack bar looks like a giant hamburger. You can also watch *Guinness World Records: Primetime*, a weekly television show, or you can visit the Guinness Internet Web site.

If you like, you can try to break a world record yourself. You don't have to be strong or fast to set a new record. You could have the world's biggest birthday party. Currently, that record is thirty-five thousand people, the number who attended a birthday party for Colonel Sanders[6] in 1979. If you have plenty of time, you can grow your hair to a record length. Hoo Sateow of Chang Mai, Thailand, whose hair is 5.15 meters long, has the current record. He stopped cutting his hair in 1929. Or you could break the record for getting into a bathtub with the most live, venomous snakes. Bibby and Rosie Reynolds-McCasland of Texas, U.S.A., hold that record now. They got into a bathtub with seventy-six live rattlesnakes.

Of course, even if you do officially break a record, you may not make it into the pages of the book. You may only get a certificate. Thousands of records are broken annually, but only a few hundred are included in the next year's book. And be careful! The Guinness corporation takes no responsibility for accidents or injuries that occur when you are making your record-breaking attempt.

Notes

1. The *Guinness Brewery* of Dublin, Ireland, has made beer since 1759.

2. A *game bird* is a kind of bird that people hunt.

3. A *pub* (short for public house) is a tavern, or a casual bar and restaurant in Britain, Ireland, and elsewhere. Friends often meet in pubs to eat, drink, and talk.

4. A *best-seller list* names the books that sell the best every week. The list appears in newspapers and magazines.

5. Jews and Christians call their holy book the *Bible*. The *Koran* is the holy book of the Islamic religion.

6. *Colonel Sanders* founded Kentucky Fried Chicken, the fast food restaurant.

After You Read

» Understanding the Reading

Answer these multiple-choice questions to see how well you understood the reading.

1. What did Sir Hugh and his friends learn in the library?

    (A) That the golden plover is faster than the grouse
    (B) That the library had very few reference books
    (C) That there was no information about game birds available
    (D) That there were no reference books listing records there

2. The Guinness Records office was established in . . .

    (A) Dublin.
    (B) London.
    (C) Southeastern Ireland.
    (D) Taiwan.

3. What type of job did the McWhirters do before starting work on *Guinness World Records*?

    (A) Publishing reference books
    (B) Making beer
    (C) Finding and checking facts
    (D) Working on their own records book

4. When was the *Guinness World Records* book first published in the U.K.?

   (A) 1951
   (B) 1954
   (C) 1955
   (D) 1956

5. In how many languages can *Guinness World Records* be read?

   (A) Thirteen
   (B) Thirty-seven
   (C) Seventy-seven
   (D) Ninety

6. Christian Adam's world record did NOT involve which of the following?

   (A) Playing the violin
   (B) Traveling 60.45 kilometers
   (C) Balancing a bicycle on his head
   (D) Riding backwards on his bicycle

7. What is special about the Guinness World Records Museum in Taiwan?

   (A) The unusual shape of some of its rooms
   (B) Its gigantic size
   (C) The fact that it was the first Guinness World Records Museum ever
       built
   (D) The huge number of exhibits it contains

8. How many poisonous snakes would you have to get into a bathtub with
   to break the current record?

   (A) 75
   (B) 76
   (C) 77
   (D) 516

≫ Vocabulary Building

Fill in the blanks in the sentences below with one of these words from the
reading.

brainchild	guide	twin	resolve	updated
injuries	reference	slim	wacky	enormous
accidents	giant	brilliant	volume	categories
unique	annually	venomous	opinion	indirectly

1. A: I can't find the Blue Dolphin Restaurant listed in the telephone book.

   B: The Blue Dolphin is a new restaurant, and that's an old phone book.
       It hasn't been _____ for over a year.

2. I can't tell Amy and her _____ sister Claire apart. They look
   exactly alike to me.

3. The character Harry Potter was the _____ of the British
   author J. K. Rowling.

4. The board of directors usually meets _____, but this year,
   they met twice.

5. A: I'm going to Italy for my vacation. Where can I get a travel
       _____? I don't know where to stay, where to eat, or
       which sights to see.

   B: You should be able to get one at any bookstore. Or you can get some
       information from the Internet.

6. Some nonpoisonous snakes closely resemble _____ snakes.

7. A: I heard Ms Szabo was in an automobile accident.

   B: Yes, and her car was totally destroyed. Luckily, her _____
       were very minor.

8. Many _____ books such as dictionaries, encyclopedias, and
   almanacs are now available on CD-ROM.

Reading Skill: Finding the Right Meaning from Context

Many English words have more than one meaning. The meanings are
usually similar, but not always. Some dictionaries do not list every meaning
of a word but only the most common definition. A dictionary cannot always
help you, but the *context* often can. You can often find the meaning of the
word from the sentence or paragraph where you see the word.

Exercise: Below are short passages from the reading. Read each one, and use the context to guess the meaning of the words in **bold**. Put an **X** by the best definition of the word.

Example:

Sir Hugh was hunting with some friends in southeastern Ireland. He shot at a kind of bird called the golden plover, but he missed. Sir Hugh said that, in his opinion, the golden plover was the fastest flying **game** bird in all of Europe.

game　　_____ (A) A contest or competition with specific rules (noun)

　　__X__ (B) Wild animals, birds, or fish that are hunted (noun or adjective)

　　_____ (C) Ready and willing (adjective)

Here is how it all started: Sir Hugh was the managing director of the Guinness Brewery. One day in 1951, Sir Hugh was hunting with some friends in southeastern Ireland. He **shot** at a **kind** of bird called the golden plover, but he **missed**. Sir Hugh said that, in his opinion, the golden plover was the fastest flying game bird in all of Europe. Some of the people in his **party** disagreed. They said that the fastest game bird was another type of bird, the grouse.

1. *shot*　　_____ (A) An injection; a vaccination (noun)

　　_____ (B) Photographed; caught on camera (past-tense verb)

　　_____ (C) Fired a gun or some other weapon (past-tense verb)

2. *kind*　　_____ (A) Sort; category; variety (noun)

　　_____ (B) Warm; generous; compassionate (adjective)

3. *missed*　　_____ (A) Felt the loss or absence of something (past-tense verb)

　　_____ (B) Didn't hit something (past-tense verb)

　　_____ (C) Was absent from some event (past-tense verb)

　　_____ (D) Didn't observe something (past-tense verb)

4. *party*　　_____ (A) A social gathering (noun)

　　_____ (B) A political group that tries to elect candidates (noun)

　　_____ (C) A group of people that gathers for a special activity (noun)

Sir Hugh had a **brilliant** idea. He realized that, every day, there are hundreds of arguments similar to the one that he had had with his friends. He also realized that many of these arguments took place in pubs and **bars** where his company's products were sold. He decided that a thorough, reliable **guide** to **records** was needed.

5. *brilliant* _____ (A) intelligent; inventive (adjective)

_____ (B) full of light; glowing; shining (adjective)

6. *bars* _____ (A) Does not allow to enter; blocks the way (verb)

_____ (B) Places where drinks are served (noun)

_____ (C) Strong metal rods (noun)

7. *guide* _____ (A) A person who directs, instructs, or informs (noun)

_____ (B) A book that gives directions or information (noun)

_____ (C) Shows the way; informs (verb)

8. *records* _____ (A) The best or top performances in some specific field (noun)

_____ (B) Musical recordings, especially ones made on vinyl discs (noun)

_____ (C) Takes notes; collects information (verb)

❯ Focus on Listening

Listen to the recording of the reading "It's a New World Record!" You will hear this reading two times. The first time, read along with the recording and focus on the speaker's pronunciation and intonation. The second time, listen for meaning. Do not look at the reading. Try to follow the ideas by listening only.

As you listen the second time, the speaker will stop occasionally and make statements about the reading. Decide if the statements are true or false. Fill in the space of the circled T or F according to what you hear and remember from the reading.

1. (T) (F)   5. (T) (F)

2. (T) (F)   6. (T) (F)

3. (T) (F)   7. (T) (F)

4. (T) (F)   8. (T) (F)

≫ Writing and Discussion Questions

Work with a partner or group to complete these questions.

1. Use the key words "Guinness World Records" to search for the Guinness Web site. Browse through the records. Read about the ones that interest you the most. Write several sentences about three of them. Share your sentences with the class. Vote on which record is the most unusual.

2. If you could set a world record in any field, what field would you choose? Why?

3. Some people believe that the *Guinness World Records* Book encourages people to do dangerous things. Should Guinness publish these kinds of records? Give reasons for your opinion.

» Crossword Puzzle

Complete the puzzle with words from the reading.

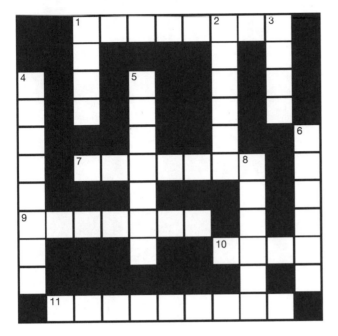

Across

1 Complete; detailed
7 One thing placed on top of another
9 Beer is made in a _____.
10 Thin; not thick
11 Intelligent; exceptional; inspired

Down

1 Norris and Ross McWhirter were _____ brothers.
2 One of a kind; special
3 Sir _____ Beaver
4 Dependable
5 Revised and modernized
6 A book, especially one that is part of a series
8 Irish city where Guinness is made

Meet Koko

Fig. 2.1 Koko.

» Warm-Up Questions

Discuss these questions in pairs or groups. Share your ideas with the class.

1. Do you believe that some animals can communicate with people? Why or why not?

2. Koko is probably the most famous gorilla in the world. What does the photo of Koko above tell you about her?

≫ Vocabulary Preview

These statements come from the reading "Meet Koko." Read each statement and then answer the questions that follow. Check your answers before you begin the reading.

Koko is a celebrity .

1. A *celebrity* is someone who is very . . .

   (A) intelligent.
   (B) experienced.
   (C) famous.

Now in her thirties, she has beautiful long black hair and piercing eyes.

2. *Piercing* eyes are eyes that . . .

   (A) seem to look through things.
   (B) are warm and gentle.
   (C) hide emotions.

Patterson asked the zoo authorities for permission to work with the young gorilla. At first, the zoo authorities refused. . . . At one year of age, Koko was healthy but was still not able to live with the adult gorillas. Patterson asked the zoo officials again if she could work with Koko.

3. Find the word in this passage that has the same meaning as *authorities* and circle it.

For example, they scream to show alarm, they make a sound like the bark of a dog to show curiosity , and they chuckle to show playfulness.

4. If gorillas show *curiosity,* they show . . .

   (A) a sense of humor.
   (B) a mixture of anger and fear.
   (C) an interest in the things around them.

5. To *chuckle* is to . . .

   (A) laugh as loud as possible.
   (B) laugh a little.
   (C) make a sound of pain.

Patterson says that the gorilla asks questions and uses abstract words such as *love* and *sadness*.

6. Which of these is another example of an *abstract* word?

(A) Kitten
(B) Bicycle
(C) Patriotism

For example, when she was given a ring, she signed "finger bracelet ."

7. A *bracelet* is normally worn . . .

(A) around the neck.
(B) around the wrist.
(C) through the ear.

Then Koko pointed to a tiny piece of red lint on the white towel and grinned at her teacher.

8. Koko *grinned* means that she . . .

(A) smiled.
(B) made an angry noise.
(C) looked confused.

The story of Koko and All Ball is told in a sentimental book for children called Koko's Kitten.

9. A book that is *sentimental* is . . .

(A) poetic.
(B) short and simple.
(C) emotional.

Gorillas may look fierce , but they are actually gentle, intelligent animals, and they can communicate better than anyone previously knew.

10. Find the word in this sentence that is OPPOSITE in meaning to *fierce* and circle it.

While You Read

Here are nine points that appear in the reading passage. There is one point for each paragraph. While you read, put the points in order from 1 to 10.

_____ Koko and All Ball
_____ Patterson first sees Koko
_____ Koko's growing vocabulary
_____ Gorilla communication skills
_____ About Koko and her accomplishments
_____ What Koko has taught the world
_____ Koko's first sign
_____ Koko's homes
_____ Koko's abstract language and humor
_____ Illness at the zoo

Meet Koko

Fig. 2.2 Koko painting.

Koko is a celebrity. Now in her thirties, she has beautiful long black hair and piercing eyes. She has been in movies and on television. She has been on the cover of magazines and has shown her paintings in museums. She has had Web casts[1] on the Internet, chatting with thousands of people. Koko's résumé is impressive for anyone, but it is even more remarkable when you consider that Koko is a 125-kilogram female gorilla.

Koko was born on July 4, 1971, at the San Francisco Zoo. She was named Hanabi-Ko (Japanese for "fireworks child"), but she has always been called Koko. Koko was three months old when

Francine "Penny" Patterson, a graduate student in psychology at Stanford University,[2] first saw her. Patterson wanted to try to communicate directly with Koko. She asked the zoo authorities for permission to work with the young gorilla.   20

3   At first, the zoo authorities refused. Soon after this, an illness spread through the gorilla population at the zoo. Koko almost died, and her mother couldn't take care of her. She had to be separated from the other gorillas. She was taken to the children's zoo,[3] and doctors and workers at the zoo took care of her there. At one year   25 of age, Koko was healthy but was still not able to live with the adult gorillas. Patterson asked the zoo officials again if she could work with Koko. This time they gave their permission.

4   Gorillas are among the best communicators of all animals. They can make a variety of sounds that have meaning. For example, they   30 scream to show alarm, they make a sound like the bark of a dog to show curiosity, and they chuckle to show playfulness. However, gorillas' vocal cords cannot make the sounds of human speech.

5   Patterson decided to teach Koko American Sign Language (ASL).[4] ASL uses hand and body movements to represent words   35 and ideas. ASL often omits words not needed for communication, such as articles and prepositions. Patterson first tried to teach Koko to make the signs for *food, drink,* and *more.* After working with Koko for about a month, Patterson was preparing some fruit for Koko's snack, and Koko made the sign for *food.* This was the first   40 time Koko communicated by signing.[5]

6   At first, Patterson taught Koko signs by taking the gorilla's hand and forming the symbol, then giving her a treat if she did it correctly. By the age of two, Koko could put signs together to form "sentences," such as "pour that hurry drink hurry." When she was   45

five, she could sign more than two hundred words. Today she signs over a thousand words and understands two thousand words of spoken English.

7   When Koko was three, Patterson was allowed to take her to Stanford University, where she was able to teach the gorilla much 50 more. In 1976, the Gorilla Foundation was established in Woodside, California, and Koko moved there. In the near future, Koko and other gorillas will move to a new home in Hawaii. This new home will be very similar to gorillas' natural habitat in Africa.

8   According to Patterson, Koko can communicate with humans. 55 Patterson says that the gorilla asks questions and uses abstract words such as *love* and *sadness*. When Koko does not know the sign for objects, she combines signs she does know to create a new compound sign. For example, when she was given a ring, she signed, "finger bracelet." Patterson says that Koko even has a sense 60 of humor. Once, one of Koko's teachers asked her about the color of a towel. Koko answered "red," although the towel was white. The teacher asked again and again. Each time, Koko signed "red" with more and more emphasis. Then Koko pointed to a tiny piece of red lint on the white towel and grinned at her teacher. 65

9
Fig. 2.3 Koko and All Ball.

In addition to her communication skills, Koko clearly has emotions. In 1984, she adopted a kitten, naming it All Ball. She treated All Ball like a baby gorilla, cuddling him in her arms and carrying 70 him on her back. She was gentle and affectionate with the cat. One day All Ball walked across a road near the gorilla compound, and a car hit him. Koko was heartbroken. Patterson asked, "Do you 75 want to talk about your kitty?"[6] Koko signed, "Cry." Patterson then asked: "What happened to your kitty?" Koko answered, "Sleep cat." When she saw a photo of All Ball, Koko pointed to the picture and signed, "Cry, sad, frown." The story of Koko and All Ball is told in a sentimental book for children called *Koko's Kitten*.   80

10   Patterson's research with Koko has taught the world an important lesson: Gorillas may look fierce, but they are actually gentle, intelligent animals, and they can communicate better than anyone previously knew.

Notes

1. A *Web cast* is a special Internet event in which a celebrity responds on-line to e-mailed questions.

2. *Stanford University*, one of the top universities in the United States, is located close to San Francisco.

3. A *children's zoo* is a section of a zoo that is interesting to children. It usually has many baby animals.

4. *American Sign Language* (ASL) is the language used by deaf people in North America and elsewhere.

5. People using ASL *sign* with this language by using hand and facial gestures rather than spoken language.

6. *Kitty* is an affectionate name for a kitten often used by children.

After You Read

» Understanding the Reading

Answer these multiple-choice questions to see how well you understood the reading.

1. Penny Patterson first saw Koko in . . .

   (A) 1970.
   (B) 1971.
   (C) 1973.
   (D) 1976.

2. When Patterson first asked zoo officials if she could work with Koko, what did the officials do?

   (A) They said that she should take Koko to Stanford University.
   (B) They permitted her to work closely with Koko.
   (C) They didn't permit her to work with Koko at all.
   (D) They refused to talk to her.

3. When she was young, Koko was not permitted to stay with other gorillas because . . .

   (A) she needed special training.
   (B) the other gorillas often fought with her.
   (C) she was sick, and her mother couldn't care for her.
   (D) she was afraid of the other gorillas.

4. Where has Koko spent most of her life so far?

   (A) In a special preserve in Hawaii
   (B) In the San Francisco Zoo
   (C) In a laboratory at Stanford University
   (D) At the Gorilla Foundation in Woodside, California

5. How do gorillas communicate curiosity?

   (A) By "barking" like a dog
   (B) By chuckling
   (C) By becoming silent
   (D) By screaming

6. What was the first word that Koko signed?

   (A) Food
   (B) More
   (C) Red
   (D) Drink

7. How many signs could Koko sign when she was five years old?

   (A) One hundred
   (B) Two hundred
   (C) One thousand
   (D) Two thousand

8. Which of these sentences would Koko most likely sign?

(A) "This towel has some red lint on it."
(B) "I'm looking forward to moving to Hawaii."
(C) "Thanks for the fruit; I enjoyed it."
(D) "All Ball pretty, Koko love."

» Vocabulary Building

Fill in the blanks in the sentences below with one of these words from the reading.

celebrity	authorities	abstract	scream	grinned
fierce	cuddling	habitat	affectionate	illness
vocal	curiosity	treat	sentimental	
résumé	heartbroken	lint	compound	

1. Lilly is a very _____ baby. She always kisses and hugs her mother and father.

2. Cats are known for their _____. They love to investigate new things.

3. A: I need a job, so I'm writing my _____.

   B: Don't forget to list all your jobs and your educational experience.

4. At one time, zoos kept most animals in small cages. Today, however, many zoos try to duplicate an animal's natural _____ as much as possible.

5. A: That woman looks familiar. Is she a _____?

   B: Yes, that's Heather Ling. She's a famous fashion model.

6. A: Have you ever seen that old movie *It's a Wonderful Life*?

   B: That's such a _____ movie! I always cry when I see it!

7. Norman Rockwell was a realist painter. He painted scenes from ordinary life, and the people in them look very real. Jackson Pollock, on the other hand, was an _____ painter. There are no recognizable figures or shapes in his paintings, just masses of color.

8. A _____ noun is composed from two shorter nouns and has a meaning different from either of the shorter words. Some examples are *earrings* and *housecat*.

Reading Skill: Identifying Word Forms

Many words in English have several forms. There may be a noun form, a verb form, an adjective form, an adverb form (although not every word has all of these forms), and sometimes others. Recognizing word forms can improve your reading comprehension and expand your vocabulary. If you recognize one word form (such as the adjective *independent*) you will recognize others (such as the noun *independence* or the adverb *independently*).

Noun forms

–ance	dominance	–dom	freedom	–ence	experience
–ery	discovery	–hood	neighborhood	–ity	electricity
–ment	commitment	–ness	cheerfulness	–ship	friendship
–sion	profession	–th	warmth	–tion	introduction

Verb forms

–ate[1]	renovate	–er	recover	
–ify	intensify	–ize	materialize	

Adjective forms

–able	remarkable	–al	seasonal	–ant	important
ate[1]	considerate	ent	confident	–ful	wonderful
ic	comic	–ical	magical	–ile	fertile
–ish	foolish	–ive	repetitive	–less	fearless
–ly[2]	lovely	–ous	mysterious	–y	snowy

Adverb forms

–ally	comically	–ly[2]	quickly

[1] Notice that *–ate* is both a verb ending and an adjective ending.

[2] Notice that *–ly* is both an adjective ending and an adverb ending.

Exercise 1: The chart below contains words from the reading. Fill in the blank spaces with the correct forms. A gray space indicates that there is no corresponding form or that the corresponding form is rare. In some cases, there may be more than one correct answer. The first one is done as an example:

Nouns	Verbs	Adjectives	Adverbs
impression	impress	impressive	impressively
		beautiful	
	communicate		
permission			
psychology			
health			
playfulness			
symbol			

Exercise 2: These statements are about Michael, a gorilla who once lived with Koko. Each has a word in an incorrect form. Underline the word that is used incorrectly, and then write the correct form on the blank line. The first one is done as an example.

Example:

Koko lived for many years at the Foundation with a gorilla named Michael. Michael was on loan to the Foundation from the Vienna Zoo. At first, his keepers were hopeful that he and Koko would mate, but their <u>relate</u> was more like that of brother and sister. ___relationship___

1. Although he was larger and stronger than Koko, he was also more fearful. The public was not allowed to visit the Gorilla Foundation partly because strangers upset Michael. When visitors appeared in his territory, he put on fierce displays. He hit on the walls and grunted to show his angry. _____

2. Michael enjoyed going out when the weather was warmth and sunny. However, when the weather was cool or rainy, he would seek the safety of the indoor shelter. _____

3. Always bright and curiosity, Michael learned over twenty signs during his first year with the Gorilla Foundation. _____

4. One morning when Michael woke up, he was extremely frightened. Through signs, he told his trainer about a terribly dream. He had dreamed of being taken prisoner when he was a baby in Africa. He made the signs for *loud noise*, *red*, and *afraid*. _____

5. In April 2000, Michael collapsed on his back. He suffered a sudden heart attack and died within minutes. Unfortunately, this is a fairly common problem of male gorillas in captive. _____

» Focus on Listening

Listen to the recording of the reading "Meet Koko." You will hear this reading two times. The first time, read along with the recording and focus on the speaker's pronunciation and intonation. The second time, listen for meaning. Do not look at the reading. Try to follow the ideas by listening only.

As you listen the second time, the speaker will stop occasionally and make statements about the reading. Decide if the statements are true or false. Fill in the space of the circled T or F according to what you hear and remember from the reading.

1. T   F   5. T   F
2. T   F   6. T   F
3. T   F   7. T   F
4. T   F   8. T   F

» Writing and Discussion Questions

Work with a partner or group to complete these questions.

1. Using the key words "Koko" or "Gorilla Foundation," visit the Foundation's Web site and try to find some information about Koko's life and accomplishments that are not given in the reading. Write or prepare a short report on the information you find.

2. Prepare a list of questions that you would like to ask Koko if you were able to interview her.

3. Think about your questions in item 2. With a partner, prepare some answers that you think Koko would be able to sign.

➤ Crossword Puzzle

Complete the puzzle with words from the reading.

Across

1 Very small piece of cloth or fabric
4 American Sign Language
5 *Hanabi-ko* means "_____ child."
7 Affectionate name for a baby cat
9 All _____, Koko's kitten
10 _____ cords are needed to speak
11 Wild; savage; vicious
12 Make a symbol for a word with a gesture

Down

2 Something good to eat
3 A place to see animals
4 Worlds like *love* and *hope* are _____ words.
6 Hugging; holding; showing affection
8 Disease; sickness

The First Modern Olympic Games

Fig. 3.1 Event from the first modern Olympic Games.

Before You Read

» Warm-Up Questions

Discuss these questions in pairs or groups. Share your ideas with the class.

1. This photograph is from the first modern Olympic Games, which were held in 1896. What kind of event is pictured?

2. What Olympic events do you enjoy watching?

3. How do you think the Olympics have changed since 1896?

≫ Vocabulary Preview

These statements come from the reading "The First Modern Olympic Games."
Read each statement and then answer the questions that follow. Check your
answers before you begin the reading.

In A.D. 393, the Roman Emperor Theodosius banned the Games because they had
become too commercial and political.

1. The word *banned* means . . .

   (A) not permitted.
   (B) avoided.
   (C) renewed.

In 1894, Coubertin organized the International Sports Congress, assembling
seventy-nine delegates from nine countries in Paris. There he suggested the revival
of the Olympics. Coubertin originally planned to hold the event in Paris. However, the
representatives convinced him to hold the Games in Greece, where the Olympics
began.

2. Find and circle the synonym for *delegates*.

3. A *revival* is a . . .

   (A) replacement.
   (B) renewal.
   (C) reduction.

The first modern Olympics were held two years later. King George of Greece opened
the Games, which attracted one hundred thousand spectators .

4. *Spectators* are people who . . . games.

   (A) play in
   (B) sell food and souvenirs at
   (C) watch

Approximately 250 athletes took part . All the athletes were male. (Women first
participated at the 1900 Olympics in Paris.)

5. Circle the word or phrase that also means *took part*.

Preparation and training for the 1896 Olympics were casual .

6. *Casual* preparation and training is . . .

   (A) demanding.
   (B) informal.
   (C) efficient.

He attended only because he was working as an accountant in Britain at the time, and some friends persuaded him to go.

7. What kind of work does an *accountant* do?

   (A) Bookkeeping
   (B) Coaching
   (C) Painting

8. His friends *persuaded* him to go. This means that they . . . him.

   (A) warned
   (B) hired
   (C) convinced

While You Read

Here are eight points that appear in the reading passage. There is one point for each paragraph. While you read, put the points in order from 1 to 8.

_____ A description of the first modern Games
_____ Casual preparation and travel for the first modern Olympics
_____ A history of the ancient Games
_____ The Olympics continue and grow
_____ Ceremonies for winners
_____ The Olympics in 2004
_____ Coubertin's dream of a revived Olympics
_____ "Accidental" participation in the Games

THE FIRST MODERN OLYMPIC GAMES

1   Every four years the best athletes gather for the Olympic Games. Athletes test their strength, endurance, and skill against competitors from nearly every nation. The modern Olympics has existed for over a hundred years. However, the Games have a much longer history than that. The ancient Olympic Games took place in Greece. Originally part of a religious festival that honored the god Zeus,[1] the first Games were first held in 776 B.C. At first, the only event was a foot race. Later, additional events were added: wrestling, boxing, discus and javelin throwing,[2] and others. The ancient Games were played for around 1,200 years. In A.D. 393, the Roman Emperor Theodosius banned the Games because they had become too commercial and political.

2   The Olympic idea was nearly forgotten until the late nineteenth century. A young French aristocrat, Baron Pierre de Coubertin, dreamed of bringing the Games back to life. He believed that it was important for young people to develop both their bodies and their minds. He also believed that international sports competitions would promote friendly relations among nations. In 1894, Coubertin organized the International Sports Congress, assembling seventy-nine delegates from nine countries in Paris. There he suggested the revival of the Olympics. Coubertin originally planned to hold the event in Paris. However, the representatives convinced him to hold the Games in Greece, where the Olympics began.

3   The first modern Olympics were held two years later. King George of Greece opened the Games, which attracted one hundred thousand spectators. Approximately 250 athletes took part. All the athletes were male. (Women first participated at the 1900 Olympics in Paris.) The athletes represented thirteen countries: Australia,

Fig. 3.1 Stadium at the first modern Olympic Games with athletes standing in rows.

Austria, Bulgaria, Denmark, France, Britain, Germany, Greece, Hungary, Italy, Switzerland, Sweden, and the United States. About half of the athletes were Greek. Coubertin wanted a mixture of ancient sports, such as running and wrestling, and modern sports, such as shooting and bicycling. There were forty-two events in nine sports.

4   The ceremonies honoring winners began at the 1896 Olympics. When an athlete won an event, musicians played the national anthem[3] of his country and his national flag was raised—still an Olympic custom. Medals were also awarded in 1896, but not until the end of the Games. Today, a gold medal is given for first place, a silver medal for second place, and a bronze medal for third. In 1896, silver was more valuable than gold, so a silver medal was given for first place and a gold for second. There was no third place award then.

5   Preparation and training for the 1896 Olympics were quite casual. Travel was slower and full of unexpected problems. For example, it took the thirteen members of the U.S. team two weeks to get to Athens, and they had to pay their own steamship fare. They thought they were going to arrive weeks early and could train in Greece. When they reached Italy, however, they learned that Greece used the Julian calendar and was two weeks ahead of most of the world. The team had to rush to Athens on a train and arrived only a day before the Games began. They had to compete with no rest or training.

6   Some athletes participated almost by accident. Australia was represented by a single runner, Edwin Flack, who won the 800- and

1,500-meter races. He attended only because he was working as an accountant in Britain at the time, and some friends persuaded him to go. J. P. Boland of Britain was in Greece on vacation when the Games began. He decided to enter the tennis event, and he won. 60

7   The first modern Olympics received little attention in international newspapers, but Coubertin was pleased and persuaded the committee to continue. Since then, the Games have been held 65 every four years except in 1916 (during World War I) and in 1940 and 1944 (during World War II). The Games have grown a great deal. At the 2000 Olympics in Sydney, Australia, there were three hundred events in twenty-eight sports. There were 10,651 competitors from 199 countries. Nearly half a million people attended the Games, and 70 up to three billion people saw some of the Games on television.

8   The 2004 Olympics will create a link with the past. For the first time since 1896, the Olympic Games will return to Athens, Greece.

Notes

1. In Greek mythology, *Zeus* was the king of the gods.

2. The *discus* is a disk, usually made of wood. The *javelin* is similar to a spear. Both are thrown as far as possible in athletic contests.

3. A *national anthem* is the official song of a nation.

After You Read

➤ Understanding the Reading

Answer these multiple-choice questions to see how well you understood the reading.

1. When were the ancient Olympics last played?

    (A) 776 B.C.
    (B) A.D. 393
    (C) A.D. 1200
    (D) A.D. 1896

2. Women first competed in the Olympic Games in . . .

(A) Paris.
(B) Athens.
(C) Sydney.
(D) Rome.

3. About how many Greek athletes took part in the first modern Olympics?

(A) 79
(B) 125
(C) 250
(D) 10,651

4. What kind of medal was given to athletes who finished first in events in 1896?

(A) A gold medal
(B) A silver medal
(C) A bronze medal
(D) No medal was given.

5. What kind of medal was given to athletes who finished third in events in 1896?

(A) A gold medal
(B) A silver medal
(C) A bronze medal
(D) No medal was given.

6. Why did the U.S. team arrive just one day before the 1896 Games began?

(A) Because their steamship arrived in Italy two weeks late
(B) Because their train broke down somewhere in Greece
(C) Because they were training in another part of Greece
(D) Because they didn't realize that Greece used another calendar

7. What event did J. P. Boland of Britain take part in?

(A) Tennis
(B) Shooting
(C) The 800-meter race
(D) The 1500-meter race

8. How many Olympic Games have been canceled since 1896?

(A) None
(B) One
(C) Two
(D) Three

» Vocabulary Building

Fill in the blanks in the sentences below with one of these words or phrases from the reading.

fare	link	anthem	took part	delegate
ancient	assembled	persuaded	accountant	casual
mixture	banned	revival	spectators	festival
urged	custom	promote	endurance	first place

1. A: There's a cheap _____ for a flight from London to Tokyo advertised on this Web site.

   B: You should make a reservation now, before the price goes up.

2. The _____ Greeks believed that Zeus and the other gods lived on Mount Olympus.

3. Auto racing is a dangerous sport, not just for the drivers but also for the _____.

4. The architecture in Barcelona is a _____ of old and new.

5. Dr. Hoffman _____ her patient to get more exercise.

6. During the Middle Ages, there was very little interest in the literature of Greece and Rome. However, during the Renaissance, there was a _____ of interest in classical writings.

7. A: Eugene, are you going to work in jeans and a sweater?

   B: I sure am. Every Friday, everyone in my office is allowed to wear _____ clothes. For one day a week, I don't have to wear a suit and tie.

8. The national _____ of Canada is a song called "O Canada."

Reading Skill: Understanding "Personal" Nouns and Terms of Origin

Recognizing personal nouns and terms of origin can improve your understanding and build your vocabulary. A "personal" noun names a person. A common suffix (ending) for personal nouns is –er. Other suffixes can also be used to form personal nouns:

–ian	–ete
–ant	–ic
–ist	–or
–ent	

The suffixes may show the activity or work that a person does. For example, a person who walks is a *walker*, a person who studies biology is called a *biologist*.

–or	actor	–ist	economist	–ic	critic
–ent	respondent	–ian	comedian	–ete	athlete
–ian	technician	–ant	attendant		

Suffixes can also show nationality—the country where someone or something comes from—or languages. They can be used to form descriptive words (adjectives).

Place name	Personal noun	Language noun	Adjective
Turkey	the Turks	Turkish	a Turkish custom
Brazil	a Brazilian		Brazilian beaches
China	the Chinese	Chinese	a Chinese city
Finland	a Finn	Finnish	Finnish food
Paris	Parisians		Parisian fashions

Exercise 1: Here are some words taken from the reading. Following the example given, form a personal noun for each word.

1. Olympics _____ Olympian _____

2. wrestling _____

3. boxing _____

4. political _____

5. athletics _____

6. competition _____

7. organize _____

8. bicycling _____

Exercise 2: Here are a number of place names taken from the reading. Fill in the blanks with related personal nouns and adjectives.

	Personal noun	Adjective
Greece	_____	_____
Britain	_____	_____
Australia	_____	_____
Austria	_____	_____
Bulgaria	_____	_____
Denmark	_____	_____
France	_____	_____
Germany	_____	_____
Hungary	_____	_____
Italy	_____	_____
Switzerland	_____	_____
Sweden	_____	_____
United States of America	_____	_____

» Focus on Listening

Listen to the recording of the reading "The First Modern Olympic Games." You will hear this reading two times. The first time, read along with the recording and focus on the speaker's pronunciation and intonation. The second time, listen for meaning. Do not look at the reading. Try to follow the ideas by listening only.

As you listen the second time, the speaker will stop occasionally and make statements about the reading. Decide if the statements are true or false. Fill in the space of the circled T or F according to what you hear and remember from the reading.

1. Ⓣ Ⓕ   5. Ⓣ Ⓕ

2. Ⓣ Ⓕ   6. Ⓣ Ⓕ

3. Ⓣ Ⓕ   7. Ⓣ Ⓕ

4. Ⓣ Ⓕ   8. Ⓣ Ⓕ

» Writing and Discussion Questions

Work with a partner or group to complete these questions.

1. The following is a list of some Olympic events or former events. Use the Internet or reference books to get information on two of them. Share the information with your class.

Summer Olympics		Winter Olympics
kayaking	handball	luge
rhythmic gymnastics	steeplechase	biathlon
synchronized swimming	taekwondo	curling
yachting	shot-put	snowboarding
pole vaulting	triathlon	giant slalom
Greco-Roman wrestling	modern pentathlon	skeleton
beach volleyball	hop, step, and jump	

2. Athens was chosen as the site for the 2004 Olympics, Beijing for the 2008 Olympics. As a group, choose the city where you want a future Olympics to be held. Search the Internet for information about the city to support your opinion. Share your group's decision with the class and explain the reasons for your choice. The class should then vote on the location of the Olympics.

3. Pierre de Coubertin believed that the Olympics helped create friendly relations between nations. Do you agree? Explain your reasons.

4. Agree or disagree: The Olympics should always be held in the same city, such as Athens. Give reasons for your choice.

5. In the past, only amateur athletes could compete in the Olympics. Today, however, many Olympic athletes are professionals. Which is better? Give reasons for your choice.

❯ Crossword Puzzle

Complete the puzzle with words from the reading.

Across

3 Arranged; made preparations

5 Site of the 2000 Olympics

8 Australian medal winner Edwin
_____

9 Site of the second modern
Olympics

10 Rebirth; renewal

12 Persuaded

Down

1 King of the ancient Greek gods

2 Type of medal given for second
place at 1896 Olympics

4 Most of the athletes at the 1896
Games were of this nationality.

6 The _____ throw is both a
modern and an ancient Olympic
event.

7 Type of medal given today for
third place

8 Transportation cost

11 Connection; joining

Business Manners Around the World

Fig. 4.1

Before You Read

➤ Warm-Up Questions

Discuss these questions in pairs or groups. Share your ideas with the class.

1. What is meant by *business manners*?

2. What are the people in the photograph above doing? Is this what business people in your country usually do when they first meet? If not, what do they do?

3. What do you think is the best way to find out about business customs of other countries?

⤜ Vocabulary Preview

These statements come from the reading "Business Manners Around the World."
Read each statement and then answer the questions that follow. Check your
answers before you begin the reading.

Your boss has sent you abroad to close an important deal .

1. To *close a deal* is to . . .

   (A) look for future customers.
   (B) successfully finish negotiations.
   (C) stop doing business with someone.

In your own country, you learn business manners bit by bit over the years, as a
child learns a language. However, when you travel overseas, you must often learn
business etiquette quickly.

2. If you do something *bit by bit,* you do it . . .

   (A) a little at a time.
   (B) over and over.
   (C) more or less correctly.

3. Circle another word in this selection that has the same meaning as
   etiquette.

In Brazil, once you've broken the ice , you may slap colleagues on the back and
touch their arms after shaking hands.

4. If you *break the ice,* you . . .

   (A) make someone feel comfortable.
   (B) do not agree with someone.
   (C) invite someone to a party.

After handshakes, it is time to exchange business cards. In Singapore and Hong
Kong, this is an especially important ritual .

5. Another word for *ritual* is . . .

   (A) requirement.
   (B) example.
   (C) ceremony.

A Korean executive said bluntly , "Without a business card, you are nobody."

6. To speak *bluntly* is to speak . . .

(A) angrily.
(B) very directly.
(C) quite briefly.

Before you go anywhere on business, you should find out if there are any cultural taboos .

7. *Taboos* are actions that are . . .

(A) forbidden.
(B) unplanned.
(C) needed.

In an Islamic country, sitting in a way that shows the soles of your feet is insulting. Writing a person's name in red ink in Korea is bad luck. Also in Korea, it is rude to place anything, even papers, on the desk of an executive you are visiting . . . In the United States and other countries, a circle formed by the thumb and forefinger signals approval, but in certain Latin and Arab countries, this is an impolite gesture.

8. There are TWO words that are close in meaning to the word *rude*. Circle them.

9. Which of these is the *forefinger?* _____

If business does take you to other countries, remember this: there are plenty of opportunities for you to make mistakes, but don't let that intimidate you.

10. Another word for *intimidate* is . . .

(A) please.
(B) frighten.
(C) delay.

While You Read

Here are six points that appear in the reading passage. There is one point for each paragraph. While you read, put the points in order from 1 to 6.

_____ An introduction to the choices and problems in international business
_____ Cultural taboos
_____ Reactions to foreigners' mistakes
_____ Business card rituals
_____ How to learn about international business manners
_____ First impressions and handshakes in different countries

BUSINESS MANNERS AROUND THE WORLD

1   Imagine that you work for an international corporation. Your   1
boss has sent you abroad to close an important deal. You arrive for
the meeting on time, and the CEO[1] and top corporate officers are
waiting. What do you do? Do you shake hands? Make eye contact?
Bow? Say "Hi"? That depends on what country you are in.   5

2   Every day, business is becoming more international. How do you
learn to make a good impression on foreign colleagues, greet them,
get to know them, and negotiate with them? In your own country,
you learn business manners bit by bit over the years, as a child learns
a language. However, when you travel overseas, you must often learn   10
business etiquette quickly. Experts suggest you spend at least thirty
hours researching the target country. Probably the best way is to
take "Business Culture 101"[2] courses taught by experienced
consultants. In addition, there are books, videos, and Internet sites
that introduce you to specific business cultures. You can also talk to   15
colleagues who have worked in the country you plan to visit.

3   Meeting and greeting rituals are important to create a positive
first impression. You may not have time to learn the language of

Fig. 4.2 Two Indian women greeting each other.

every country where you do business, but you can at least learn to say "Good morning" and "How are you?" Everyone appreciates the time that you take to learn a few polite greetings. The next question is whether to shake hands. Nowadays, in most countries, it is safe to shake hands—not too firmly, not too lightly—and make brief eye contact with everyone you meet. Some business people from the United States greet a large number of people with a "group wave"[3] in place of individual handshakes, but many business people don't appreciate this. Even in Japan and Korea, where people traditionally greet each other with a bow, a handshake is acceptable and sometimes even preferred when greeting international visitors. You may greet an Indian businessperson with a *namaste*. Place both palms together at chest level and then bow. You may use a similar greeting called the *wai* when in Thailand, or you may shake hands and then place one hand over your heart. In Brazil, once you've broken the ice, you may slap colleagues on the back and touch their arms after shaking hands.

Fig. 4.3 International executives exchanging business cards.

After handshakes, it is time to exchange business cards. In Singapore and Hong Kong, this is an especially important ritual. Holding your card in both hands, present it to each person at a meeting, starting with the most senior. Place your card in front of the person with the print facing him or her. When a card is presented to you, look it over. Don't put it in your wallet or back pocket, and don't write on it. Business cards and the rituals of exchanging them are important all over Asia. A Korean executive said bluntly, "Without a business card, you are nobody." 55

5 Finally, learning what to avoid is also important. Before you go anywhere on business you should find out if there are any cultural taboos. In an Islamic country, sitting in a way that shows the soles of your feet is insulting. Writing a person's name in red ink in Korea is bad luck. Also in Korea, it is rude to place anything, even 60 papers, on the desk of an executive you are visiting. Never touch an Indonesian on the head. In Taiwan, never wrap a gift in white paper, and never give a clock as a gift. In the United States and other countries, a circle formed by the thumb and forefinger signals approval, but in certain Latin and Arab countries, this is an 65 impolite gesture.

6 If business does take you to other countries, remember this: there are plenty of opportunities for you to make mistakes, but don't let that intimidate you. Business people around the world tolerate foreigners' mistakes more than those of their fellow citizens. 70 Their reaction to your mistakes will more likely be amusement than anger. If you watch what others do, ask questions, and keep an open mind, you can succeed anywhere.

Notes

1. A *CEO*, or Chief Executive Officer, is the highest officer of many corporations.

2. *Business Culture 101* means a basic class in business culture. The number "101" refers to beginning-level university courses. It is used informally to indicate a beginning course on any topic.

3. Some people wave and say hello to everyone at a meeting all at one time rather than greeting each one individually. This is a *group wave*.

After You Read

❯ Understanding the Reading

Answer these multiple-choice questions to see how well you understood the reading.

1. What does the author think is the best way to learn international business manners?

   (A) By taking classes taught by experts
   (B) By visiting Internet sites
   (C) By watching videos
   (D) By talking to friends

2. How many hours should you spend researching business culture before you visit another country?

   (A) At least 1
   (B) At least 10
   (C) At least 30
   (D) At least 101

3. The *namaste* is a common form of greeting in . . .

   (A) Brazil.
   (B) Hong Kong.
   (C) Taiwan.
   (D) India.

4. When is it all right to slap someone on the back after shaking hands in Brazil?

   (A) After bowing
   (B) After an argument
   (C) After establishing friendly relations
   (D) After several years of friendship

5. What do you do when a business card is presented to you in Hong Kong?

   (A) Put it in your wallet
   (B) Write the date on it
   (C) Read it
   (D) Place it in your back pocket

6. Which action would be rude in Korea?

   (A) Writing your name on a check
   (B) Opening a map on the desk of an executive you are visiting
   (C) Forming a circle with your forefinger and thumb
   (D) Handing papers to a senior executive at a meeting

7. What does the circle gesture mentioned in paragraph 6 mean in the United States?

   (A) Approval
   (B) Anger
   (C) Insult
   (D) Embarrassment

8. What point is made in the last paragraph of the reading?

   (A) That you should try not to make mistakes in international business
   (B) That you can't learn the business manners of every country
   (C) That people forgive mistakes from foreigners more than those of people from their own country
   (D) That business etiquette is becoming less and less important

» Vocabulary Building

Fill in the blanks in the sentences below with one of these words or phrases from the reading.

imagine	ritual	forefinger	gesture	greet
eye contact	shake	taboos	amusement	tolerate
nowadays	slap	intimidate	approval	etiquette
first impression	bow	negotiate	colleagues	abroad

1. A: Mr. Park, I would like you to meet some of the people that I work with.

   B: Of course, I'd be happy to meet your _____.

2. When I was a child, I used to _____ scoring the winning goal in a World Cup match.

3. In the past, it was common for students in the U.K. to study classical languages such as Latin and Greek. _____, it is more common for them to study modern languages.

4. My _____ of Joan was not very positive, but soon I realized what a wonderful person she was.

5. The clerk at the toy store said this puzzle would provide hours of _____ for a four year old, but my child put it together in five minutes.

6. The tea ceremony is an important _____ in Japan.

7. Professor Jordan's math class is very difficult, but don't let that _____ you. If you take it, you'll learn a lot about calculus.

8. Would you rather attend a university in your own country or go to school _____?

Reading Skill: Skimming

Skimming is reading quickly to find the main idea. You can skim an article, a Web page, a newspaper, a textbook chapter, or a whole book. Why should you use this method? You skim if you are in a hurry, have a lot to read, or need to review something you read previously. You also skim to judge if certain material is worth reading.

Here's one basic method of skimming: First, read the first and last paragraphs, or introduction and conclusion. Next, read the first and last sentence of each paragraph. Finally, look for key words and read those parts.

Above all, read quickly: about three to four times your normal speed. Don't try to comprehend more than about 50% of the material. Don't try to understand details, and do not let unfamiliar vocabulary slow you down.

Exercise: Skim the passage below in four minutes. Then answer the questions that follow. Chart your time.

Beginning time: _____

Business Dining

1   Business people in Denmark will often invite you to join them for dinner. This meal, called middag, is served from 6 to 8 P.M. It is the main meal of the day. Danish executives may invite you to join them at a restaurant; in Copenhagen, the city's many basement cafés are popular spots for business meals. However, it is also quite common for Danes to invite you to dine in their homes. If your spouse is traveling with you, he or she will probably be invited as well.

2   If you are invited into a Danish home, it is customary to bring a gift. Flowers are always appreciated, but do not bring white flowers as those

are associated with mourning. Other popular gifts are chocolates and desk items with your company logo on them.

3   The host and hostess at Danish dinner parties sit at opposite ends of the table. The female guest of honor is seated to the right of the host, and the male guest of honor to the right of the hostess. Name cards are often used for other guests.

4   The traditional Danish dinner party begins with soup, which is followed by a seafood appetizer. After that is the main meat course, often served with a salad, and finally dessert. Wine or beer often accompanies dinner. Or there may be a smorgasbord, a large table of seafood, sausages, breads, vegetables, and desserts served buffet-style. This style of serving is often used at larger dinner parties.

5   You should use your silverware in the European style, with the fork in your left hand and the knife in your right. Food is cut with the knife, and the knife and fork never switch hands. Bring the food to your mouth with the tines of your fork pointing downward. Take only foods that you are sure you will enjoy, and don't take more than you think you can eat, because leaving food on your plate may offend your host and hostess. When you have finished, place your fork and knife parallel on the right side of the plate.

6   A Danish dinner party customarily begins with the host toasting the guest of honor. Do not drink from your glass before this toast has been offered, and if the host stands, so should you. At the end of the meal, the male guest of honor is expected to toast the hostess. A typical toast is "Skal!"

7   It is not uncommon for dinner parties to last until 1 a.m. in the summer and 10:30 or 11 P.M. in the winter. After dinner, your host may ask you to stay for coffee and drinks and even invite you for a walk before the party is over. Be sure to thank your host and hostess before departing.

Ending time: _____

Questions

1. Who is the audience for this passage (be specific)?

_____

2. What is the purpose of this passage?

_____

3. Which paragraph is about using your knife and fork?

_____

≫ Focus on Listening

Listen to the recording of the reading "Business Manners Around the World." You will hear this reading two times. The first time, read along with the recording and focus on the speaker's pronunciation and intonation. The second time, listen for meaning. Do not look at the reading. Try to follow the ideas by listening only.

As you listen the second time, the speaker will stop occasionally and make statements about the reading. Decide if the statements are true or false. Fill in the space of the circled T or F according to what you hear and remember from the reading.

1. T   F   5. T   F
2. T   F   6. T   F
3. T   F   7. T   F
4. T   F   8. T   F

≫ Writing and Discussion Questions

Work with a partner or group to complete these questions.

1. This reading discusses several ways to get information about business cultures in other countries. Which way do you think is best? Why? What are other ways to get information on international business cultures? Describe them.

2. Choose two of the business activities below, and discuss the etiquette for doing these activities in your culture. With a partner, write dialogs for these two activities.

greeting a visitor	exchanging business cards
introducing your colleagues to a visitor	having a meeting with visiting executives
inviting a visitor to a meal	negotiating a business deal
giving gifts	

3. Using the Internet, research some of the activities in question 2 above. Find out the etiquette for them in at least one other culture.

4. What are some business taboos in your culture? Write a short paragraph describing some activities that foreign business persons should avoid.

» Crossword Puzzle

Complete the puzzle with words from the reading.

Across

2 Bend at the waist as a form of greeting

5 Overseas; in another country

6 Forbidden things

9 Manners; polite behavior

10 Red _____ is unlucky in Korea.

11 Place to carry money, credit cards, photographs, etc.

Down

1 Chief Executive Officer

2 Directly; openly; honestly

3 Thai gesture of greeting

4 Indian gesture of greeting

7 _____ the ice (establish friendly relations)

8 Ceremony, rite

The World's Most Popular Monster

Fig. 5.1 Godzilla.

Before You Read

Warm-Up Questions

Discuss these questions in pairs or groups. Share your ideas with the class.

1. This picture is from the first Godzilla movie. Have you ever seen a Godzilla movie, or heard of Godzilla? What do you know about him?

2. Do you enjoy monster movies? Why or why not?

Vocabulary Preview

These statements come from the reading "The World's Most Popular Monster." Read each statement and then answer the questions that follow. Check your answers before you begin the reading.

Godzilla is a frightening creature . . . .He is awakened by nuclear weapons testing, and he wakes up in a bad mood . The monster attacks Tokyo again and again, and many people die.

1. If someone is *in a bad mood,* he or she is . . .

    (A) angry and upset.
    (B) in danger.
    (C) completely confused.

2. Circle the phrase that means *monster.*

In both, the two monsters disappear into the sea. However, Godzilla is apparently the winner of the fight in the Japanese version. In the U.S. version, King Kong seems to be the victor .

3. If something is *apparently* true, it . . .

    (A) seems to be true.
    (B) will be true in the future.
    (C) is certainly true.

4. Circle a synonym for *victor.*

Later Godzilla movies were made for a younger audience, and the movies are not as scary as the original. The third movie, *Godzilla vs. Mothra* (1964), features a giant moth, which is frightening only if you own a giant sweater.

5. Circle a synonym for *scary.*

In most of these movies, Godzilla and his monster friends fight alien creatures who invade Earth. Godzilla eventually became . . . well, silly. . . . Director Ichiro Honda objected to the idea of making Godzilla ridiculous , and he retired from making Godzilla movies for many years.

6. Another word for *invade* is . . .

    (A) visit.
    (B) attack.
    (C) help.

7. Find a synonym for *ridiculous* and circle it.

Like the original, this Godzilla has no regard for private or public property and destroys many landmarks .

8. If a person *has no regard for* property, he or she does not . . .

(A) own any property.
(B) have any understanding of it.
(C) care if it is damaged.

9. In this sentence, *landmarks* means . . .

(A) well-known buildings.
(B) vehicles.
(C) other monsters.

Not only is Godzilla the most recognizable giant monster in the world, but he (or she) also has staying power .

10. If something has *staying power*, it . . .

(A) is large and strong.
(B) lasts a long time.
(C) seldom travels.

While You Read

Here are seven points that appear in the reading passage. There is one point for each paragraph. While you read, put the points in order from 1 to 7.

_____ A description of the first Godzilla movie
_____ The funny, friendly Godzilla of the sequels
_____ The second Godzilla movie
_____ The future of Godzilla
_____ A summary of Godzilla's different aspects
_____ Why the original *Godzilla* was a serious movie
_____ The Hollywood Godzilla

THE WORLD'S MOST POPULAR MONSTER

1   Godzilla has destroyed Tokyo several times, but he has also   1
saved it from alien creatures. He has been killed in many different
ways, but he keeps returning. He stands 50 meters tall, he has sharp
teeth and claws, and he breathes fire, but he is not always a
frightening monster. Sometimes he is friendly, sometimes even   5
funny.

2   Godzilla first appeared in 1954 in Japan, in the movie *Gojira*.
Like all Japanese Godzilla films, *Gojira* was made by Toho
Studios. The name *Gojira* is a combination of the English word
gorilla and *kujira*, the Japanese word for whale. It came from the   10
nickname of a large, tough-looking employee of Toho Studios. The
movie was released in the United States in 1956 as *Godzilla: King
of the Monsters*. Filmed in black and white, this first film is very
somber. Godzilla is a frightening creature, a giant prehistoric
reptile that resembles *Tyrannosaurus rex*.[1] He is awakened by   15
nuclear weapons testing, and he wakes up in a bad mood. The
monster attacks Tokyo again and again, and many people die. The
actors in the movie seem truly terrified when he attacks the city.
In Japan, the United States, and elsewhere, *Godzilla: King of the
Monsters* made audiences hide under their seats.   20

3   The dark tone of the first movie comes from the director, Ishiro
Honda, who was a soldier during World War II. Honda was
strongly affected by the use of atomic bombs at the end of the war.
"Science never produces just happiness, it also produces the
opposite, as Godzilla shows," he once said. The director wanted the   25
Godzilla movie to warn the world of the dangers of nuclear testing
and nuclear war.

4   The second film in the series, *King Kong vs. Godzilla* (1962), features the most famous monster from the West, a giant gorilla, fighting the top monster of the East. The Japanese version and the 30 U.S. version of this movie are exactly the same until the final scene. In both, the two monsters disappear into the sea. However, Godzilla is apparently the winner of the fight in the Japanese version. In the U.S. version, King Kong seems to be the victor.

5   Godzilla became so popular that there were many more 35 sequels. Later Godzilla movies were made for a younger audience, and the movies are not as scary as the original. The third movie, *Godzilla vs. Mothra* (1964), features a giant moth,[2] which is frightening only if you own a giant sweater. Godzilla's personality changed too. Beginning with *Ghidrah, the Three Headed Monster* 40 (1965), he becomes a more-or-less helpful monster. In most of these movies, Godzilla and his monster friends fight alien creatures who invade Earth. Godzilla eventually became . . . well, silly. In one movie his fiery breath turns into smoke rings. In another, he learns to speak. In *Godzilla vs. Monster Zero* (1969), he even dances! 45 Director Ichiro Honda objected to the idea of making Godzilla ridiculous, and he retired from making Godzilla movies.

Fig. 5.2 Godzilla fights a giant plant in one of the "silly" Godzilla movies.

Meanwhile, Toho Studio's budget for special effects[3] got smaller and smaller. The 50 monsters were operated mainly by "suitimation." In other words, an actor put on a rubber monster suit. In sequels such as *Godzilla vs. the Smog Monster* (1972) the 55 acting is poor, and so is the language dubbing.[4]

Fig. 5.3 Godzilla in New York City.

In 1998, Godzilla was reinvented by Hollywood. Modern computerized special effects were used in place of "suitimation." In this movie, Godzilla travels to New York City. Like the original, this Godzilla has no regard for private or public property and destroys many landmarks. However, this Godzilla is larger (over 65 meters) and faster than the original monster. Furthermore, the new Godzilla is not male but female, and she lays eggs that hatch into baby godzillas. By the end of the movie, Mama Godzilla and all her babies are destroyed—all but one.

Not only is Godzilla the most recognizable giant monster in the world, but he (or she) also has staying power. Over twenty-two sequels have been made. Will there be more Godzilla movies? Who knows? That last baby Godzilla might grow up!

Notes

1. A *Tyrannosaurus rex* was a large, meat-eating dinosaur.

2. A *moth* is an insect similar to a butterfly. Young moths, called larvae, eat fabrics such as wool and cotton.

3. *Special effects* are techniques that movie makers use to make things that happen in a movie seem real. For example, special effects would be needed to create the illusion that a monster is attacking a city. Today most special effects are created with computers.

4. *Language dubbing* is a method of adding a translation to a movie soundtrack. For example, if an Italian movie is dubbed into English, the actors seem to be speaking English even though they originally spoke their lines in Italian.

After You Read

⟫ Understanding the Reading

Answer these multiple-choice questions to see how well you understood the reading.

1. The name *Gojira* comes from the . . .

   (A) Japanese word for gorilla.
   (B) nickname sailors use for a whale.
   (C) name of an American monster.
   (D) nickname of an employee at Toho Studios.

2. What is Mothra?

   (A) A large insect
   (B) A giant gorilla
   (C) A whale
   (D) A three-headed monster

3. How are the U.S. version and the Japanese version of the second Godzilla movie different?

   (A) The U.S. version is longer.
   (B) The Japanese version is more serious.
   (C) King Kong, not Godzilla, seems to win the fight in the U.S. version.
   (D) In the U.S. version, both monsters are destroyed.

4. In which of these movies does Godzilla change his personality?

   (A) *Godzilla vs. Monster Zero*
   (B) *Ghidrah, the Three Headed Monster*
   (C) *King Kong vs. Godzilla*
   (D) *Godzilla vs. the Smog Monster*

5. Which does the author find the most ridiculous?

   (A) Godzilla fighting aliens
   (B) Godzilla dancing
   (C) Godzilla talking
   (D) Godzilla smoking

6. Which statement best describes sequels such as *Godzilla vs. the Smog Monster*?

   (A) It is nearly impossible to see them today.
   (B) There are no English language versions of these movies.
   (C) Their quality is not very good.
   (D) They have great special effects and wonderful acting.

7. What did the monster in the original movie have in common with the monster in the 1998 Hollywood movie?

(A) They were the same height.
(B) They were both males.
(C) They both visited Tokyo.
(D) They were both destructive.

8. How many baby godzillas survived in the 1998 movie?

(A) None
(B) One
(C) Twenty-two
(D) Hundreds

⟩ Vocabulary Building

Fill in the blanks in the sentences below with one of these words or phrases from the reading.

somber	version	apparently	claws	staying power
feature	tough-looking	prehistoric	victor	terrifying
alien	nickname	retired	sequels	landmark
objected	invade	grow up	creature	employee

1. There were two _____ to the hit movie *The Matrix*: one was *The Matrix Reloaded*, and the other was *The Matrix Revolutions*.

2. One of the most important inventions was the wheel, but no one knows who invented it because it happened in _____ times.

3. The Eiffel Tower is the most famous _____ in Paris.

4. The Rolling Stones have more _____ than most musical groups. They have been performing since the early 1960s.

5. When my father turned sixty-five, he _____, and now he spends most of his time playing golf.

6. My brother saw the movie *Dracula* when he was a child. It was so _____ that it gave him bad dreams for months.

7. Some of Robert Parker's books have tough male detectives as the main characters, but some of his novels _____ a tough female detective named Sunny Randall.

8. All the members of the cat family have sharp teeth and _____.

Reading Skill: Understanding Passive Sentences

Passive sentences are sometimes confusing for readers. You must read passive sentences carefully to identify the true subject, or performer, of the action.

Verbs in English can be either active or passive. In an active sentence, the subject *performs* the action of the main verb. In a passive sentence, the subject *receives* the action. A passive verb has two parts: (1) an auxiliary verb, which is a form of "to be," and (2) a past-participle main verb.

Passive verbs are not as direct or strong as active verbs. However, there are two important uses of passive verbs:

1. To emphasize the receiver of the action

   This type of sentence usually has a *by* phrase that tells you the true performer of the action.

   Active: Ishiro Honda *directed* the first movie.
             (This sentence puts more emphasis on Ishiro Honda)

   Passive: The first movie *was directed* by Ishiro Honda.
             (This sentence puts more emphasis on the first movie.)

2. When the performer is unknown or not important.

   When the author does not know who performs the action or does not consider the performer important. This type of sentence never has a *by* phrase.

   The movie *was released* in the United States in 1956.
   (The author doesn't know who released it or doesn't think it is important to mention who released it.)

Exercise 1: Read the sentences below. If the author uses a passive verb in the sentence for the first reason given above (to emphasize the receiver of the action), mark that sentence **1**. If the author uses a passive verb for the second reason (the performer is unknown or not important), mark that sentence **2**.

_____ 1. The music for the first Godzilla movie was composed by Akira Ifukube.

_____ 2. The name Gojira was chosen because that was the nickname of a large, tough-looking employee of the studio.

_____   3. The creature was often portrayed by an actor in a rubber suit.

_____   4. Godzilla was reinvented by Hollywood.

_____   5. Most of the Godzilla movies have been dubbed into English.

Exercise 2: Rewrite the following sentences. Change active sentences to passive and passive sentences to active.

1. The monster was awakened by nuclear testing.

   _____

2. In the first movie, Godzilla terrifies the people of Tokyo.

   _____

3. In the Japanese version of the second movie, King Kong is apparently defeated by Godzilla.

   _____

4. Many alien creatures invade Earth in the Godzilla sequels.

   _____

5. Audiences were not frightened by Mothra.

   _____

➤ Focus on Listening

Listen to the recording of the reading "The World's Most Popular Monster." You will hear this reading two times. The first time, read along with the recording and focus on the speaker's pronunciation and intonation. The second time, listen for meaning. Do not look at the reading. Try to follow the ideas by listening only.

As you listen the second time, the speaker will stop occasionally and make statements about the reading. Decide if the statements are true or false. Fill in the space of the circled T or F according to what you hear and remember from the reading.

1. Ⓣ Ⓕ   5. Ⓣ Ⓕ

2. Ⓣ Ⓕ   6. Ⓣ Ⓕ

3. Ⓣ Ⓕ   7. Ⓣ Ⓕ

4. Ⓣ Ⓕ   8. Ⓣ Ⓕ

≫ Writing and Discussion Questions

Work with a partner or group to complete these questions.

1. Using the Internet, search for more Godzilla movie sequels. Choose three or four and write short descriptions of them.

2. In the sequels, Godzilla fights a giant gorilla, a three-headed monster, a giant moth, and a smog monster. Imagine other monsters Godzilla might fight. What do they look like? Where do they come from? What happens when they fight Godzilla?

3. Some people say that sequels to movies are almost never as good as the original movies. Do you agree? Why or why not?

4. Audiences in 1954 found the original Godzilla movie very frightening. Would this movie be so frightening today? Why or why not?

5. If you can, rent a Godzilla movie. Stop the movie now and then, and explain in English what is happening. If you watch it with classmates, share opinions after the movie is finished.

❯ Crossword Puzzle

Complete the puzzle with words from the reading.

Across

1 The Japanese name for Godzilla

4 A method used to animate Godzilla

5 Mothra is a huge _____.

7 Winner

10 A three-headed monster

11 The Godzilla movie had more than twenty-two _____.

Down

2 From another planet; extraterrestrial

3 King _____ is a giant gorilla.

4 Dark; depressing

6 Eggs _____ and baby animals come out.

8 Godzilla has sharp teeth and _____.

9 *Tyrannosaurus* _____

A Brief History of Coffee

Fig. 6.1 Kaldi and his goats.

Before You Read

Warm-Up Questions

Discuss these questions in pairs or groups. Share your ideas with the class.

1. Do you like coffee? Why or why not?

2. Look at the picture on this page. Try to guess how it is connected to the topic of the reading.

3. When do you think coffee was discovered? Skim paragraph 2 of the reading to find out if your guess is correct.

⫸ Vocabulary Preview

These statements come from the reading "A Brief History of Coffee." Read each statement and then answer the questions that follow. Check your answers before you begin the reading.

Coffee is a popular beverage , one of the most popular in the world today. . . . Where did this drink come from?

1. Circle another word in this statement that has the same meaning as
    beverage.

One day, while Kaldi was napping , his goats were grazing in a mountain meadow.

2. In the sentence above, what was Kaldi doing?

    (A) Sleeping
    (B) Guarding the goats
    (C) Thinking

3. What were the goats doing?

    (A) Drinking water
    (B) Running
    (C) Eating plants

The animals ate some red berries on shiny green plants. Kaldi woke to find them acting frisky and dancing around the meadow.

4. If an animal is *frisky*, it is . . .

    (A) sick and slow-moving.
    (B) playful and energetic.
    (C) comical and silly.

The beans were soaked in water to make them soft, and the monks drank the liquid and ate the beans for energy.

5. The beans were . . . in water.

    (A) cooked for a short time
    (B) grown
    (C) allowed to sit for a long time

Babi Budan, an Indian merchant, secretly carried fertile plants from Arabia to India and started his own coffee plantation. In 1616, Dutch merchants smuggled cuttings from coffee plants out of Aden and started coffee plantations in southeast Asia.

6. *Fertile* plants are . . .

(A) rare and valuable.
(B) able to create new plants.
(C) only used for trading.

7. Find a phrase that means *smuggled*. Circle it.

In 1827, Brazilian diplomat Francisco Palheta went to French Guiana to negotiate a treaty.

8. Which of these is a *diplomat?*

(A) A general
(B) A merchant
(C) An ambassador

When they said goodbye, she gave him a bouquet of flowers. Hidden among the blossoms were cuttings from a coffee plant.

9. Circle another word for *blossoms.*

Espresso, a thick, strong coffee made with steam , was introduced by Luigi Bezzara in 1901.

10. *Steam* is . . . .

(A) the gas produced by heating water.
(B) hot milk.
(C) ice-cold water.

While You Read

Here are nine points that appear in the reading passage. There is one point for each paragraph. While you read, put the points in order from 1 to 9.

_____ Coffee developments in the twentieth century
_____ The birth of the Brazilian coffee industry
_____ Coffee's spread to the Middle East
_____ The popularity of coffee and questions about its origin
_____ The end of the coffee-growing monopoly
_____ Coffee in Britain and its colonies
_____ The discovery of coffee
_____ The lasting impact of Kaldi's discovery
_____ Coffee comes to Vienna

A Brief History of Coffee

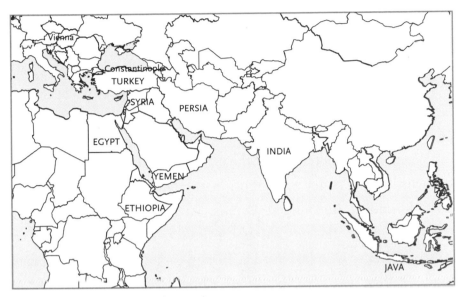

Fig. 6.2 Part of the eastern hemisphere.

1   Coffee is a popular beverage, one of the most popular in the world today. East and West, there are people who cannot start their day without their morning cup. Where did this drink come from? How long have people drunk it? The answers may surprise you.

2   Coffee dates back at least to the sixth century. It comes from the country of Ethiopia. According to one legend, coffee was discovered by Kaldi, a goat herder. One day, while Kaldi was napping, his goats were grazing in a mountain meadow. The animals ate some red berries[1] on shiny green plants. Kaldi woke to find them acting frisky and dancing around the meadow. Boldly, he ate some of the berries himself. Soon, he felt alert and full of energy. Believing it was a miracle, he took the berries to a nearby monastery.[2] Chadely, the abbot, tried the berries. He realized that they could help the monks stay awake during late-night prayers. The monks began drying the beans and sending them to distant monasteries. The beans were soaked in water to make them soft, and the monks drank the liquid and ate the beans for energy.

3   Sometime before the twelfth century, traders carried coffee from Africa to Arabia. The plants were first grown in Yemen. The drink's popularity then spread into Egypt, Syria, Persia, and Turkey. 20 In 1575, the world's first coffee shop, Kiv Han, opened in Constantinople (Istanbul). Coffee shops became an important part of Middle Eastern life. People visited them to talk, play chess, and listen to music and poetry, just as they do today.

4   Warriors and merchants of the Ottoman Empire[3] helped spread 25 the word about coffee to Europe. In the late seventeenth century, Turkish armies surrounded Vienna, Austria, and unsuccessfully tried to capture the city. After the attack, Franz Kolschitzky, an Austrian officer who had lived in Turkey, found bags of "dried black fodder"[4] that was actually coffee. Kolschitzky opened a café in 30 Vienna in 1683. The Viennese began the custom of sweetening coffee and adding milk.

5   Coffee arrived even earlier in London. The first coffee houses opened in the 1640s. London coffee houses became centers of discussion known as "penny universities." They also were places to 35 do business. Opened in 1668, Edward Lloyd's Coffee Shop attracted insurance agents. It became Lloyd's of London, the world-famous insurance company. Coffee spread to Britain's North American colonies and cafés opened in Boston, Philadelphia, and New York City in the 1690s. By 1700, coffee was more popular than beer as a 40 morning drink in New York City. After the Boston Tea Party[5] of 1773, drinking coffee was an act of patriotism in the colonies.

6   For many centuries, the coffee plant was grown only in the Middle East. Arab coffee merchants carefully guarded their monopoly. There were strict laws against exporting coffee plants; 45 only the dried beans could be traded. That changed in 1600. Babi Budan, an Indian merchant, secretly carried fertile plants from Arabia

to India and started his own coffee plantation. In 1616, Dutch merchants smuggled cuttings[6] from coffee plants out of Yemen and started coffee plantations in southeast Asia. Coffee growing in Java 50 was so successful that the word *java* became a synonym for coffee.

7 It was romance that brought coffee to Brazil. The story began in 1783 when the Dutch gave French King Louis XIV a coffee plant. It is believed that 80% of today's coffee plants are descendants of that plant. Cuttings were taken to France's tropical colonies, including 55 French Guiana. In 1827, Brazilian diplomat Francisco Palheta went to French Guiana to negotiate a treaty. While he was there, he developed a relationship with the wife of the French governor. When they said goodbye, she gave him a bouquet of flowers. Hidden among the blossoms were cuttings from a coffee plant. These 60 cuttings were the source of the huge Brazilian coffee industry.

8 In the twentieth century, there were many advances in coffee making and marketing. In 1900, the Hills Brothers Company began vacuum-packing[7] coffee in cans. The next year, Japanese- 65 American scientist Satori Kato of Chicago invented instant coffee. In 1903, Ludwig Roselius introduced a brand of decaffeinated 70 coffee which he named Sanka. In 1938, scientists from the Nestlé Corporation in Switzerland invented freeze-dried coffee. Espresso, 75 a thick, strong coffee made with steam, was introduced by Luigi Bezzara in 1901, and

Fig. 6.3 South America.

Fig. 6.4 A modern coffee shop.

in 1946, Achilles Gaggia invented an easy-to-use espresso machine. In 1971, a coffee shop named Starbucks opened in Pike Place Market[8] in Seattle, and created a new market for high-priced espresso drinks. In the 1980s, coffee shops in Korea, Taiwan, and Japan multiplied. They became popular places for young couples and groups to meet.

If Kaldi walked into a modern coffee shop he would probably be amazed that the beans that he and his goats discovered almost 1,500 years ago had such an impact on world culture.

Notes

1. *Berries* are small fruits that grow from bushes (strawberries, blackberries). The "fruit" of the coffee bush (which are also called coffee beans) are not really berries, but they look like them.

2. A *monastery* is a place where religious people called *monks* go to pray and think. The chief monk is sometimes called an *abbot*. Monks and monasteries are common to a number of the world's great religions.

3. The Ottoman Empire was a large, powerful Turkish empire. At one time it ruled most of the Middle East as well as parts of the Mediterranean region and southeastern Europe.

4. *Fodder* is food for animals, such as horses and cows.

5. *The Boston Tea Party* was a protest against British rule in the American colonies. The British placed a high tax on tea. Colonials dressed as American Indians went on board British ships and threw the tea into Boston Harbor.

6. *Cuttings* are pieces of plants that can be used to grow other plants. Cuttings are a way to grow new plants without seeds.

7. *Vacuum-packing* is a process of putting foods like coffee in cans while removing excess air. The absence of air prevents spoiling and keeps the food fresh.

8. *Pike Place Market* is a historic marketplace in Seattle. It is well known for its fresh fish and fruit as well as for its cafés and restaurants.

After You Read

» Understanding the Reading

Answer these multiple-choice questions to see how well you understood the reading.

1. Outside of Ethiopia, coffee was first grown in . . .

   (A) Turkey.
   (B) India.
   (C) Yemen.
   (D) Java.

2. What coffee-drinking custom began in Vienna?

   (A) Coffee was first served warm there.
   (B) People first drank coffee at cafés rather than at home there.
   (C) Espresso was invented there.
   (D) People began adding sugar and milk to coffee there.

3. What did most New Yorkers drink in the morning before 1675?

   (A) Beer
   (B) Tea
   (C) Milk
   (D) Coffee

4. Eighty percent of all coffee plants grown today come from a coffee plant that was . . .

   (A) taken from Arabia to India.
   (B) taken from Aden to Java.
   (C) given to King Louis XIV.
   (D) given to Francisco Palheta.

5. Why did Francisco Palheta originally go to French Guiana?

   (A) To steal coffee plants
   (B) To arrange a treaty
   (C) To see the governor's wife
   (D) To learn how to grow coffee plants

6. Instant coffee was invented in . . .

   (A) 1900.
   (B) 1901.
   (C) 1902.
   (D) 1903.

7. Who developed decaffeinated coffee?

(A) The Hills Brothers
(B) Satori Kato
(C) Ludwig Roselius
(D) Luigi Bezzara

8. According to the author, what would Kaldi's reaction probably be if he walked into a coffee house today?

(A) Surprise
(B) Anger
(C) Embarrassment
(D) Pleasure

» Vocabulary Building

Fill in the blanks in the sentences below with one of these words from the reading.

beverage	napping	alert	surrounded	strict
smuggling	bouquet	grazing	miracle	discussion
exporting	romance	thick	legend	steam
soaked	monopoly	descendants	multiplied	amazed

1. The chemical in coffee and tea that makes one feel _____ is called caffeine.

2. A milk shake is a _____ drink made from ice cream, flavored syrup, and milk.

3. Henry couldn't answer the professor's question because he had been _____ in class.

4. A: Rudolfo, what did you buy your wife for your wedding anniversary?
   B: I bought her a _____ of twelve red roses.

5. All dogs alive today are _____ of wild wolves.

6. Akiko was _____ when she won the lottery. She couldn't believe her good luck.

7. The police broke up a gang of criminals who were _____ cigarettes into the country.

8. James Watt invented an engine that ran on _____. It used wood to heat water, and then the water vapor turned wheels.

Reading Skill: Understanding Chronological Order

This reading is a history of coffee. Like all histories, it emphasizes *time*, or when events happened. In some cases the author provides specific times (*in 1971, in the late sixteenth century*). In other cases, you see words that explain the order of events (*after that, before this, soon, then, later*). Finally, some time words or phrases indicate that things happen at the same time (*when, while, as, meanwhile*).

In some readings, chronological order is strictly followed. Events are listed or discussed exactly in the order in which they occurred. However, in other histories—including this one—some events are listed out of order.

Exercise 1: Look at these selections from the reading and do the following:

A. Circle words or phrases that give specific times of events.

B. Draw one line under words or phrases that give a *sequence* of events.

C. Draw two lines under words or phrases that show two events occurring *at the same time*.

1. Sometime before the twelfth century, traders carried coffee from Africa to Arabia. The plants were first grown in Yemen. The drink's popularity then spread into Egypt, Syria, Persia, and Turkey. In 1575, the world's first coffee shop, Kiv Han, opened in Constantinople (Istanbul).

2. By 1700, coffee was more popular than beer as a morning drink in New York City. After the Boston Tea Party of 1773, drinking coffee was an act of patriotism in the colonies.

3. In 1827, Brazilian diplomat Francisco Palheta went to French Guiana to negotiate a treaty. While he was there, he developed a relationship with the wife of the French governor. When they said goodbye, she gave him a bouquet of flowers.

Exercise 2: Order these cities according to the time coffee houses first appeared in them. Number the cities 1 to 4. Then copy the sentence or sentences that helped you discover your answer.

_____ Vienna

Sentence(s) _____

_____

_____ New York City

Sentence(s) _____

_____

_____ Constantinople

Sentence(s) _____

_____

_____ London

Sentence(s) _____

_____

Question: Are the appearance of coffee houses in these cities given in strict chronological order in the reading?   Yes No

❯ Focus on Listening

Listen to the recording of the reading "A Brief History of Coffee." You will hear this reading two times. The first time, read along with the recording and focus on the speaker's pronunciation and intonation. The second time, listen for meaning. Do not look at the reading. Try to follow the ideas by listening only.

As you listen the second time, the speaker will stop occasionally and make statements about the reading. Decide if the statements are true or false. Fill in the space of the circled T or F according to what you hear and remember from the reading.

1. Ⓣ Ⓕ   5. Ⓣ Ⓕ

2. Ⓣ Ⓕ   6. Ⓣ Ⓕ

3. Ⓣ Ⓕ   7. Ⓣ Ⓕ

4. Ⓣ Ⓕ   8. Ⓣ Ⓕ

⟫ Writing and Discussion Questions

Work with a partner or group to complete these questions.

1. Do you think the story about Kaldi told in this reading is true? Why or why not?

2. Using the Internet, try to find information on when coffee was first introduced to your country.

3. Many people around the world prefer coffee to tea. For a class report, interview at least three people who are NOT in your class to find out which (if either) they prefer. Explain their reasons.

4. Here are some quotations (sayings) about coffee. Choose three of them and explain what they mean.

   "If this is coffee, please bring me some tea; but if this is tea, please bring me some coffee."
   —Abraham Lincoln

   "Good communication is as stimulating as black coffee, and just as hard to sleep after."
   —Anne Morrow Lindbergh

   "If brains were money, you'd need to take out a loan to buy a cup of coffee."
   —Shelley Long (actress on the television show *Cheers*)

   "Good coffee is like friendship: rich and warm and strong."
   —Unknown

   "Do you know how helpless you feel if you have a full cup of coffee in your hand and you start to sneeze?"
   —Jean Kerr

   "A mathematician is a device for turning coffee into theorems."
   —Paul Erdos

   "No matter how much strong black coffee we drink, almost any after-dinner speech will counteract it."
   —Kin Hubbard

   "Coffee should be as black as hell, as strong as death, and as sweet as love."
   —Turkish proverb

» Crossword Puzzle

Complete the puzzle with words from the reading.

Across

2 Chain of coffee shops

5 Take something illegally across a border

8 Sheep who are eating grass are _____.

9 Occupy; take control of

11 Indonesian island, and another word for coffee

12 Legendary discoverer of coffee

Down

1 Energetic; lively; playful

3 Something to drink

4 First coffee house, _____ Han

6 French _____, a territory in South America

7 Inventor of a simpler espresso machine, Achilles _____

10 Seattle attraction, _____ Place Market

The Amazing Mr. Tesla

Fig. 7.1 Tesla with electrical equipment.

Before You Read

» Warm-Up Questions

Discuss these questions in pairs or groups. Share your ideas with the class.

1. What famous inventors do you know about? What did they invent?

2. Nikola Tesla was a great inventor, but he was not famous. Look at the reading quickly to find some of the things he invented. What do you think was his most significant invention?

❱ Vocabulary Preview

These statements come from the reading "The Amazing Mr. Tesla." Read each statement and then answer the questions that follow. Check your answers before you begin the reading.

His mother had little formal education, but she learned books of poetry by heart and invented kitchen gadgets .

1. If you learn poetry *by heart*, you . . .

   (A) learn to speak it in an emotional way.
   (B) memorize it.
   (C) learn to write it.

2. *Kitchen gadgets* are . . .

   (A) instructions and recipes for cooking food.
   (B) stories about spirits that live in the kitchen.
   (C) small tools for cooking and working in the kitchen.

He met with the electrical genius Thomas Edison.

3. This sentence says that Edison was . . .

   (A) brilliant.
   (B) wealthy.
   (C) only a beginner.

However, Tesla believed that Edison cheated him and Tesla left the company in anger in 1885. The two men became bitter rivals .

4. Two people are *bitter rivals* when they . . .

   (A) have a lasting friendship.
   (B) are in an unfriendly competition.
   (C) ignore each other completely.

He promoted the use of alternating current (AC) electricity and he developed motors and generators for using AC. Edison, on the other hand, championed the use of direct current (DC)

5. Circle another word in this sentence that is close in meaning to *championed*.

This competition is known as "the battle of the currents." In fact, AC is better than DC, especially when electricity must travel long distances. Tesla got a contract to provide AC electricity for the Chicago World's Fair. This helped him win the struggle against Edison.

6. There are TWO words in these sentences that are close in meaning to the word *battle*. Circle both of them.

He accidentally created a giant display of artificial lightning, and once he knocked out the power system for Colorado Springs.

7. If the power system is *knocked out*, it . . .

(A) does not work.
(B) is suddenly turned on.
(C) is more powerful than usual.

Newspaper reporters ridiculed him for this.

8. The reporters . . . him.

(A) praised
(B) interviewed
(C) made jokes about

Tesla was certainly a genius, but he was an eccentric genius. . . . He always carefully cleaned the silverware before eating in restaurants, and ate only boiled food. After a taxicab accident in 1937, his behavior became even more unusual.

9. Circle the word that is a synonym for *eccentric*.

10. Which of these are examples of *silverware*?

(A) Rings, bracelets, and necklaces
(B) Cups and glasses
(C) Knives and forks

While You Read

Here are nine points that appear in the reading passage. There is one point for each paragraph. While you read, put the points in order from 1 to 9.

_____ Tesla's childhood
_____ More inventions and plans for inventions
_____ Tesla in Colorado Springs
_____ Tesla's strange habits
_____ Tesla meets Edison
_____ Why Tesla was not well known
_____ Tesla inventions in the 1890s
_____ Introduction to Tesla, the "unknown inventor"
_____ The Battle of the Currents

THE AMAZING MR. TESLA

1   Who invented the x-ray and the neon light? The speedometer   1
and remote control vehicles? The answer is Nikola Tesla. Who?
Nikola Tesla, the greatest inventor you probably never heard of.

2   Nikola Tesla was born in the small town of Smiljan in Croatia[1]
in 1856. He was born, appropriately, during an electrical storm. His   5
father was a church official and a mathematician. His mother had
little formal education, but she learned books of poetry by heart
and invented kitchen gadgets. Nikola was only five when he created
his first invention, an engine powered by twelve beetles.

3   At the Polytechnic School in Gratz, Tesla studied the new   10
science of electrical engineering. In 1884, after working briefly in
Budapest and Paris, he went to the United States. He had four
cents and a letter of recommendation in his pocket when he got
off the ship in New York City. He met with the electrical genius
Thomas Edison.[2] The letter, written by one of Edison's European   15

associates, read, "My Dear Edison: I know two great men and you are one of them. The other is this young man!" Edison hired Tesla, and Tesla developed several inventions for Edison's company. However, Tesla believed that Edison cheated him and Tesla left the company in anger in 1885. The two men became 20 bitter rivals.

4   Tesla opened his own laboratory in New York City. He promoted the use of alternating current (AC) electricity and he developed motors and generators for using AC. Edison, on the other hand, championed the use of direct current (DC) and tried to 25 convince the public that AC electricity was dangerous and expensive. This competition is known as "the battle of the currents." In fact, AC is better than DC, especially when electricity must travel long distances. Tesla got a contract to provide AC electricity for the Chicago World's Fair.[3] This helped him win the struggle 30 against Edison. Today the electrical energy used by homes and businesses everywhere is AC electricity.

5   The 1890s was a very creative period for Tesla. He experimented in several areas, including radio. Most people believe Marconi invented radio, but it was Tesla who developed the basic 35 equipment needed for radio broadcasting. Tesla also invented an x-ray machine, a neon light, and a remote-controlled boat. Unfortunately, many of his plans and inventions were 40 destroyed in a fire in his laboratory in 1895.

6

Fig. 7.2 Tesla's generator at his lab in Colorado Springs.

In 1899, Tesla moved to Colorado Springs,[4] where he built a strange laboratory. 45

He tried to develop a machine that would broadcast electrical power wirelessly, like radio waves. He accidentally created a giant display of artificial lightning, and once he knocked out the power system for Colorado Springs. However, he was basically unsuccessful. While in Colorado Springs, he also said that he heard radio messages from Mars and Venus. Newspaper reporters ridiculed him for this. In fact, the inventor had made an important discovery. The radio signals that he had detected were created by distant stars.

7   For the next few decades, Tesla continued to invent and develop ideas for future inventions. During World War I, he invented a type of radar to hunt German submarines. He created plans for the laser, the microwave oven, and the electron microscope. He invented a "death ray" that he thought could destroy airplanes from hundreds of miles away. He believed that this device—later known as a particle-beam weapon—would make war impossible.

8   Tesla was certainly a genius, but he was an eccentric genius. He was afraid of women's pearl jewelry. He refused to stay in a hotel room with a number that was divisible by the number three. He always carefully cleaned the silverware before eating in restaurants, and he ate only boiled food. After a taxicab accident in 1937, his behavior became even more unusual. He spent most of his time feeding pigeons in the park and taking care of injured pigeons in his room at the Hotel New Yorker.

9   A brilliant inventor of over seven hundred devices, Tesla spoke nine languages and had a photographic memory. Nevertheless, he was not a good businessman or self-publicist. Despite Tesla's contributions to technology, he died penniless and almost unknown in 1943.

Notes

1. *Croatia* is today an independent nation in southeast Europe. At the time of Tesla's birth, it was part of the Austro-Hungarian Empire.

2. *Thomas Edison* is the well known inventor of the light bulb and other important devices.

3. The *Chicago World's Fair* was a large international exposition held in Chicago in 1893.

4. *Colorado Springs* is a city in the western United States.

After You Read

» Understanding the Reading

Answer these multiple-choice questions to see how well you understood the reading.

1. It is "appropriate" that Tesla was born during an electrical storm because he . . .

   (A) spent much of his life working with electricity.
   (B) had a stormy, difficult life.
   (C) had a loud, violent nature, like an electrical storm.
   (D) had a lifelong fear of thunder and lightning.

2. What provided the power for the first engine that Tesla built?

   (A) Chemicals
   (B) Insects
   (C) Batteries
   (D) Birds

3. Tesla was NOT successful at which of these?

   (A) Winning the "battle of the currents"
   (B) Opening his own laboratory
   (C) Detecting radio signals from distant stars
   (D) Transmitting electrical power without wires

4. What was Tesla's relationship with Edison after 1885?

   (A) They competed strongly against each other.
   (B) Edison worked for Tesla.
   (C) They were close business associates and friends.
   (D) They often cooperated despite their dislike of each other.

5. What does the author say about the fire of 1895?

(A) It was deliberately set by supporters of Edison.
(B) It was caused by artificial lightning.
(C) It proved that AC electricity was dangerous.
(D) It destroyed Tesla's inventions and plans.

6. Which of these did Tesla believe could stop war?

(A) Radar
(B) Particle beam weapons
(C) Radio controlled boats
(D) Lasers

7. Which of these was Tesla afraid of?

(A) Room 13 at a hotel
(B) Boiled food
(C) Women's pearl earrings
(D) Pigeons

8. What did Tesla have in common with his mother?

(A) Both of them invented electrical generators.
(B) Both of them had good memories.
(C) Neither of them had any formal education.
(D) Neither of them ever lived in Croatia.

❯ Vocabulary Building

Fill in the blanks in the sentences below with one of these words or phrases from the reading.

recommendation	jewelry	penniless	boiled	broadcast
remote control	gadgets	appropriately	eccentric	knocked out
formal education	rivals	contributions	bitter	divisible
championed	struggle	power system	poetry	genius

1. Alice inherited a diamond ring, an emerald necklace, and other valuable _____ from her grandmother.

2. Airplanes called drones don't require pilots. They can be operated by _____.

3. A: When you applied for a job here, who did you ask to give you letters of _____?

   B: I asked one of my university teachers and one of my old bosses.

4. Nelson Mandela, the former president of South Africa, _____ human rights.

5. Baseball games were first _____ on radio in the 1920s.

6. The number 12 is _____ by 2, 3, 4, and 6.

7. A: My aunt is very _____. As a matter of fact, she thinks that she is a chicken.

    B: How terrible! Have you taken her to a doctor?

    A: Oh, no, we enjoy getting fresh eggs from her every morning!

8. My friend Joy is _____ named. She is the most joyful person I know.

Reading Skill: Understanding Vocabulary from Context

If you see a word that you do not know in a reading, you can often use the words around it—the context—to guess the meaning of the word. Mastering this skill gives you three advantages. One, it helps you save time because you are not looking up every unfamiliar word in a dictionary. Two, it sharpens comprehension; examining the context improves your general understanding of the text. Three, it helps you build vocabulary.

Here are three ways to find the meaning of a word from its context:

1. Look for synonyms or explanations of the unfamiliar word.

2. Look for examples that explain the unfamiliar word.

3. Use your general knowledge to guess the meaning of the unfamiliar word.

Exercise: Read the following passage and guess the meaning of the highlighted words. Give a definition or synonym for each word in the blanks at the end of the reading. Explain your choices to the class.

When Tesla returned from Colorado to the East Coast in 1900, he wrote an article for *Century Magazine* in which he unveiled a plan for a futuristic transmitting tower and power station, which he called the World Broadcasting System. He planned to use this tower to link the world's telephone and telegraph systems and to send messages, news, pictures, weather reports, and even electrical power all over the world. The story got

Fig. 7.3 Tower at Wardenclyffe.

the attention of the wealthy financier J. P. Morgan, who invited Tesla to his daughter's gala wedding reception. Morgan agreed to finance the tower. Tesla chose a site near Wardenclyffe, Long Island.

The tower consisted of a 55-meter steel framework with a huge steel sphere on top of it. This huge metal ball was designed to tap the power of the sun. Morgan, however, only provided $150,000; Tesla needed $1,000,000. Labor problems and a national recession slowed work. His sponsor Morgan refused to invest more money, and Tesla could not find another backer. In 1905, the project had to be abandoned. The failure to build this tower was Tesla's greatest disappointment.

Tesla continued to conduct experiments at Wardenclyffe for several years. When there was a huge, unexplained explosion in Siberia in 1908, some people suggested that it was caused by Tesla sending energy through the Earth's core. For many years, visitors to the Wardenclyffe area wondered what the purpose of the curious, unfinished structure could be.

1. unveiled _____

2. link _____

3. gala _____

4. sphere _____

5. tap _____

6. backer _____

7. core _____

8. curious _____

≫ Focus on Listening

Listen to the recording of the reading "The Amazing Mr. Tesla." You will hear this reading two times. The first time, read along with the recording and focus on the speaker's pronunciation and intonation. The second time, listen for meaning. Do not look at the reading. Try to follow the ideas by listening only.

As you listen the second time, the speaker will stop occasionally and make statements about the reading. Decide if the statements are true or false. Fill in the space of the circled T or F according to what you hear and remember from the reading.

1. (T) (F)   5. (T) (F)

2. (T) (F)   6. (T) (F)

3. (T) (F)   7. (T) (F)

4. (T) (F)   8. (T) (F)

» Writing and Discussion Questions

Work with a partner or group to complete these questions.

1. These are some of the inventions that Tesla worked on. Using the Internet, get more information on two or three of these technological devices. Find out how they were developed, how they work, and what they are used for.

electron microscopes	rotary engines	automobile	lasers
microwave ovens	vacuum tubes	neon lights	x-rays
remote control vehicles	ignition systems	speedometers	radar

2. Which of these devices do you think are most important today? Why?

3. Both Thomas Edison and Nikola Tesla were geniuses. Today Edison is famous but Tesla is almost unknown. Why do you think some people become famous and some do not? Decide the most important factors: talent, luck, money, connections, or determination.

4. If you had the choice of being wealthy or famous, which would you choose? Why?

5. If you could invent a machine or device to do anything, what would it be? Explain.

❧ Crossword Puzzle

Complete the puzzle with words from the reading.

Across

1 Completely without money
4 Competitors
5 Tesla invented the _____ light.
8 Direct current
9 Tesla believed he heard radio signals coming from here.
10 Fight; battle
11 Alternating current
12 Tesla's death-ray was a _____ -beam weapon.

Down

2 _____ Tesla
3 Eating utensils
6 Thomas _____ was an electrical genius.
7 Small devices

The ABCs of Hangul

Fig. 8.1 King Sejong.

Before You Read

» Warm-Up Questions

Discuss these questions in pairs or groups. Share your ideas with the class.

1. This reading is about *Hangul*, the Korean alphabet. What do you think is the relationship between this topic and the picture on this page?

2. What other alphabets are you familiar with? Give examples.

❯ Vocabulary Preview

These statements come from the reading "The ABCs of Hangul." Read each statement and then answer the questions that follow. Check your answers before you begin the reading.

Ask a Korean to name something uniquely Korean, and you will probably get a variety of answers.

1. If something is *uniquely* Korean, it . . .

   (A) is only partly Korean.
   (B) was originally Korean, but is now universal.
   (C) belongs especially to Koreans and to no one else.

Some will say their food, especially the spicy national dish Kimchee.

2. A *spicy* dish is one that . . .

   (A) has strong flavors.
   (B) is a traditional food.
   (C) is eaten with almost every meal.

Some will say their reliable , stylish industrial products.

3. Another word for *reliable* is . . .

   (A) inexpensive.
   (B) dependable.
   (C) attractive.

Linguists say that it belongs to the same language family as Mongolian, Hungarian, Turkish, and Finnish.

4. *Linguists* study . . .

   (A) customs.
   (B) languages.
   (C) politics.

From the fifth century, Korean was written in Chinese characters .

5. In this sentence, *characters* means . . .

   (A) the people in a play or book.
   (B) personalities.
   (C) symbols for letters and numbers.

Unfortunately, the Idu writing system was very complicated. To read and write Idu, one had to learn thousands of intricate characters.

6. Circle a synonym for *intricate*.

He ruled during a period of great economic, cultural, and political development in Korea, an era known as the Golden Age .

7. Circle TWO words that mean *age*.

He founded *Chiph-yon-jon*, a royal academy of scholars. This institute published books on history, geography, agriculture, and medicine.

8. Circle the word that is closest in meaning to *academy*.

An enlightened ruler, the king wanted all Koreans to be able to read and write, and he wanted the Korean language to have its own alphabet.

9. The word *enlightened* is closest in meaning to . . .

(A) progressive.
(B) powerful.
(C) experienced.

Korean children learn to write at an early age, and illiteracy is almost unknown.

10. *Illiteracy* is . . .

(A) bad behavior.
(B) an uncooperative attitude.
(C) the inability to read and write.

While You Read

Here are eight points that appear in the reading passage. There is one point for each paragraph. While you read, put the points in order from 1 to 8.

_____ A description of Hangul
_____ The creation of Hangul
_____ Hangul Day
_____ Hangul, a uniquely Korean creation
_____ The old Korean writing systems
_____ The slow process of adopting Hangul
_____ Introducing King Sejong
_____ The results of adopting Hangul

THE ABCs OF HANGUL

1   Ask a Korean to name something uniquely Korean, and you will probably get a variety of answers. Some will say their food, especially the spicy national dish *kimchee*.[1] Some will say their traditional medicine, *hanyak*. Some will say their reliable, stylish industrial products. However, many will say their alphabet: the simple, elegant writing system known as *Hangul*.

2   The Korean language is thousands of years old. Linguists say that it belongs to the same language family as Mongolian, Hungarian, Turkish, and Finnish. Korean also has Chinese influences. From the fifth century, Korean was written in Chinese characters. There were several systems of writing Korean, but the most successful was *Idu*, which added special symbols to the Chinese characters to indicate Korean verb endings. Unfortunately, the Idu writing system was very complicated. To read and write Idu, one had to learn thousands of intricate characters. Only scholars could master it.

3   King Sejong the Great is the father of the modern alphabet system. Sejong became king in 1418. He ruled during a period of great economic, cultural, and political development in Korea, an era known as the Golden Age. Sejong was a swordsman, an astronomer, a poet, a musician, and a scholar. He founded the *Chiph-yon-jon*, a royal academy of scholars. This institute published books on history, geography, agriculture, and medicine.

4   An enlightened ruler, the king wanted all Koreans to be able to read and write, and he wanted the Korean language to have its own alphabet. Sejong once said that using Chinese characters to express ideas in Korean was like trying to fit a square tool into a round hole. Along with the academy, he began a ten year project to design an

easily learnable alphabet. When they completed their work in 1443, the king published a proclamation called *Hun-Min-Jeong-Eum* ("Correct Sounds to Instruct the People"). In this document, the king wrote that "because Chinese characters are a foreign writing system, they cannot truly capture Korean meaning. Common people have no way to express their thoughts and feelings. Therefore, we have created a set of twenty-eight letters. The letters are easy to learn, and it is our hope that they will improve the lives of the people." The new alphabet later became known as *Hangul* (or *Han-gul*, or *Hangeul*) meaning "great letters."

Fig. 8.2 Hun-Min-Jeong-Eum document.

Unlike Chinese, Hangul is a phonetic language: each sign represents a sound. And unlike English, in which each letter may have several sounds, the pronunciation of the Korean letters is very regular. Originally, Hangul had twenty-eight letters, but only twenty-four are used today. There are three basic vowels, shaped like the three most important elements in Taoist[2] thought: sky, earth, and humanity. The symbol for the sky is a dot, the symbol for earth a horizontal line, and the symbol for humanity a vertical line. The other vowels are created by adding strokes to these basic symbols. The shape of the five basic consonants is based on the shape of the mouth and tongue when the sound is pronounced. Other consonants are variations on these five consonants. Letters are grouped into "syllable blocks." Each syllable block contains up to four letters and begins with a consonant. Each consonant is followed

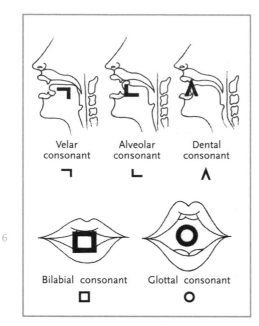

Velar consonant   Alveolar consonant   Dental consonant

ㄱ   L   Λ

Bilabial consonant   Glottal consonant

☐   O

Fig. 8.3 Basic consonant shapes of the mouth and tongue.

6

by one or two vowels, and sometimes there is a final consonant. Korean can be written in vertical columns from top to bottom and right 65 to left or in horizontal rows running from left to right.

King Sejong created an easily learnable alphabet. However, not everyone 70 accepted Hangul immediately. Scholars who had spent years learning *Hanja* (the Korean word for Chinese characters) especially disliked the new alphabet. They referred to Hangul as 75 "morning letters" because the alphabet could be learned in a single morning. Sometimes they called it "women letters" because, at that time, only males could be scholars. For centuries, Hangul was mainly used by people of lower social status. In the nineteenth and twentieth centuries, most Koreans used a writing system that 80 combined Chinese characters and Hangul. Since World War II, however, Hangul has become more and more popular in South Korea, and, in 1949, North Korea outlawed the use of Hanja altogether.

7   The use of Hangul has had some remarkable results. Korean 85 children learn to write at an early age, and illiteracy is almost unknown. Moreover, because Hangul is a phonetic alphabet, it is better suited for computer keyboards and computer programs than a pictograph-based language. A fifteenth-century alphabet has helped Korea in the global marketplace. 90

8   Understandably, Hangul is a source of Korean pride. For many
years, on October 9, the nation celebrated "Hangul Day." Many
people were disappointed when the government recently decided
that Hangul Day would no longer be celebrated as an official
national holiday. Others outside Korea were disappointed also. In   95
fact, there are many people worldwide who think that Hangul is a
wonderful invention, and that October 9 should be celebrated
everywhere as World Linguistics Day.

Notes

1. The popular Korean dish *kimchee* is made of cabbage and seasonings.

2. *Taoist* (pronounced *Daoist*) thought is a philosophical and religious
   system of beliefs that originated in China. It dates from the fourth
   century B.C.

After You Read

> Understanding the Reading

Answer these multiple-choice questions to see how well you understood the
reading.

1. Which statement about Idu is NOT true?

   (A) It was based on Chinese characters.
   (B) It was very difficult to learn.
   (C) It used special markers to indicate Korean verb endings.
   (D) It was the only method used to write Korean in Chinese characters.

2. King Sejong said that using Chinese characters to express ideas in Korean
   was like trying to fit a square tool into a round hole. He could have said
   also that it was like . . .

   (A) watching fish swim in a river.
   (B) using salt to make your food taste sweet.
   (C) using a horse to pull a cart.
   (D) growing cabbage to make *kimchee*.

3. How many letters are used in Hangul today?

   (A) Three
   (B) Five
   (C) Twenty-four
   (D) Twenty-eight

4. Which of these represents one of the correct ways to read Hangul?

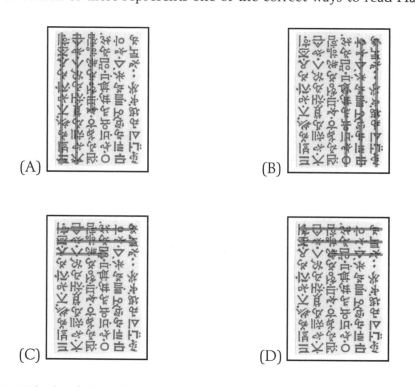

(A)   (B)

(C)   (D)

5. Which of the following is IMPOSSIBLE in a Hangul syllable block?

   (A) The block begins with a vowel.
   (B) The second character is a vowel.
   (C) One vowel follows another vowel.
   (D) The block ends with a consonant.

6. Why was the Hangul alphabet called "women letters?"

   (A) The letters were invented by women.
   (B) Women could not become scholars, and most could not read Chinese
       characters, so they used Hangul.
   (C) Scholars thought that some of the Hangul characters had feminine
       shapes.
   (D) At first, King Sejong and the academy did not permit males to use
       Hangul characters.

7. What is the Korean term for Chinese characters?

(A) *Hanyak*
(B) *Han-gul*
(C) *Hangeul*
(D) *Hanja*

8. What decision did the Korean government recently make about Hangul Day?

(A) To urge other nations to celebrate it as World Linguistics Day
(B) To make it a national holiday
(C) To celebrate it on a day other than October 9
(D) To no longer celebrate it as an official holiday

➤ Vocabulary Building

Fill in the blanks in the sentences below with one of these words from the reading.

uniquely	linguists	intricate	stroke	elegant
enlightened	spicy	influences	master	column
symbol	illiteracy	reliable	characters	era
status	phonetic	vertical	express	academy

1. The government is training hundreds of new reading teachers in order to reduce the _____ rate in the country.

2. _____ believe that there are about six thousand languages spoken in the world today.

3. To show the number five, you can draw four vertical lines and one diagonal _____.

4. A: Do you like bland foods or _____ foods?

   B: I prefer hot foods like Indian curry.

5. Paul studied Arabic for a year but was never able to _____ the language.

6. Your password must have four _____. They may be either numbers or letters.

7. The bookkeeper used a calculator to add up the long _____ of figures.

8. Spanish is a _____ language. Each letter always represents the same sound.

Reading Skill: Understanding Patterns of Organization

Information in English is often organized into various patterns. Each pattern reflects a certain purpose, or a way of thinking about the subject. A single pattern can be used to organize information into a paragraph, an essay, or even an entire book. Often, however, in longer readings, a variety of patterns are mixed. Here are some of the most common patterns, their purposes, and examples of how they might be introduced in a paragraph or reading.

Pattern	Purpose	Example
Problem/Solution (Question/Answer)	To offer answers to a problem or question.	What can be done to stop world hunger? One way is to stop wasting food.
Process	To explain a method or the way that something has happened or is made by breaking it down into steps, stages, or a sequence of events.	There are five easy steps to buying a good used car.
Comparison	To show how two or more things are alike.	The educational systems in Japan and China are similar in some ways.
Contrast	To show how two or more things are different.	Now let's see how the educational systems of Japan and China are different.
Definition	To give the precise meaning or significance of a concept or thing.	What is democracy? It is rule by majority.
Persuasion	To make readers believe something or do something.	We should try harder to find a cure for cancer.

Pattern	Purpose	Example
Narration	To give the sequence of events or tell a story.	The discovery of King Tut's tomb is an exciting story. It began in 1891.
Description	To give information about the physical appearance of an object or details about the nature of a concept.	This article will take you on a tour of the Taj Mahal, the most beautiful monument in India
Cause	To give reasons why some event happens or why some condition exists.	Why is the sea salty? There are several reasons.
Effect	To explain the result of some event. (Cause and effect are often, but not always, combined.)	There were several interesting results of the eruption of the Krakatoa volcano.
Examples	To identify some things that illustrate a type of thing or concept.	Most large corporations have similar structures. Let's consider the giant oil company Exxon, for example.
Analysis	To separate a system or a concept into parts and examine each part individually.	What elements are needed to create a good television series? What role does each of these elements play?
Classification	To show how a person, place, thing, or idea fits into a category or group of similar persons, places, things, or ideas. (Classification often includes definitions.)	How does the gorilla fit into the animal kingdom? First of all, the gorilla is a mammal.

Exercise 1: Answer the following questions about patterns of organization in the reading. Write the number of the paragraph where you found your answer on the first blank line, then write the answer from the reading on the second line.

1. Which paragraph uses *classification?* _____

   What does the author classify? _____

2. Find a paragraph that contains *contrast.* _____

   What does the author contrast? _____

3. Which paragraph contains an *example?* _____

   What is it an example of? _____

4. Which paragraph contains an *effect?* _____

   What effects are given? _____

5. Which paragraph contains *description?* _____

   What is described? _____

Exercise 2: Below is a list of titles of readings. Decide which organizational patterns would probably be used to organize the information in each reading and write the name of the pattern in the blank. Several answers are possible for each title.

1. "The Regional Dialects of the Korean Language"

   _____

2. "The Two Systems of Writing Japanese: *Kana* and *Kanji*"

   _____

3. "Come On, Let's Learn Some Chinese!"

   _____

4. "How to Make *Kimchee*"

   _____

5. "Legends of King Sejong"

   _____

6. "Musical Instruments of Vietnam"

   _____

» Focus on Listening

Listen to the recording of the reading "The ABCs of Hangul." You will hear this reading two times. The first time, read along with the recording and focus on the speaker's pronunciation and intonation. The second time, listen for meaning. Do not look at the reading. Try to follow the ideas by listening only.

As you listen the second time, the speaker will stop occasionally and make statements about the reading. Decide if the statements are true or false. Fill in the space of the circled T or F according to what you hear and remember from the reading.

1. Ⓣ Ⓕ   5. Ⓣ Ⓕ
2. Ⓣ Ⓕ   6. Ⓣ Ⓕ
3. Ⓣ Ⓕ   7. Ⓣ Ⓕ
4. Ⓣ Ⓕ   8. Ⓣ Ⓕ

» Writing and Discussion Questions

Work with a partner or group to complete these questions.

1. *Kimchee* and Hangul are two uniquely Korean things. What are some things that you believe are unique to another country?

2. Using the Internet, find information about two of the following alphabets; then share your information with the class. Write several sentences about each of the alphabets you choose. Copy examples of words written in the alphabet you choose.

Arabic	Hebrew	Thai	Cherokee
Ancient Egyptian	Japanese	Urdu	Cyrillic
Ancient Greek	Russian	Tibetan	Farsi (Persian)

3. Imagine that you are a member of a United Nations committee for world holidays. In small groups, decide which events should be celebrated and choose the best day for the celebration. Report your ideas to the class and then vote for the best suggestions.

» Crossword Puzzle

Complete the puzzle with words from the reading.

Across

1 Letters and numbers
5 Scientists who study language
6 A system of writing Korean using Chinese characters
7 An institute for learning and study
10 Well designed; stylish
11 Horizontal lines
12 Learn completely
13 Korean king, father of Hangul

Down

2 Korean alphabet
3 Flavorful; hot tasting
4 Not able to read or write
8 Vertical lines
9 Age; time period

Doctors Without Borders

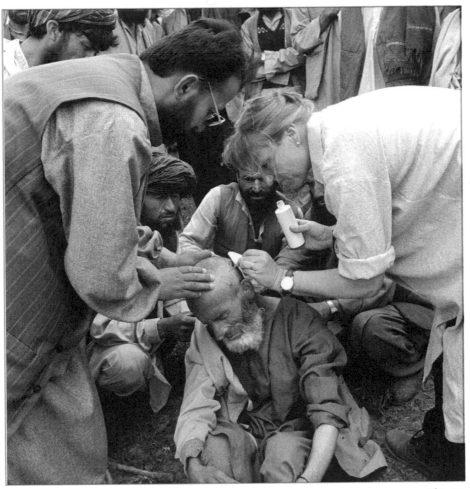

Fig. 9.1

Before You Read

» Warm-Up Questions

Discuss these questions in pairs or groups. Share your ideas with the class.

1. This reading is about an organization that is often called MSF. Read the title and skim the first paragraph of the reading. Why does the organization use those initials? What is another name for this organization?

2. Look at the photograph on this page. What is happening? Describe some of the ways doctors give aid.

❯ Vocabulary Preview

These statements come from the reading "Doctors Without Borders." Read each statement and then answer the questions that follow. Check your answers before you begin the reading.

The philosophy of MSF is that all people have the right to medical care, regardless of race, religion, or nationality.

1. This sentence tells us that everyone deserves medical care . . .

    (A) because of their race, religion, or nationality.
    (B) no matter what race, religion, or nationality they are.
    (C) especially designed for people of their race, religion, and nationality.

MSF began as "a couple of doctors with a suitcase and a dream." Now it is the largest nongovernmental organization for emergency medical relief .

2. A synonym for *relief* is . . .

    (A) aid.
    (B) equipment.
    (C) training.

MSF sends teams not only to locations that are in the spotlight but also to places where forgotten wars continue to cause suffering.

3. If a location is *in the spotlight*, it is . . .

    (A) well liked.
    (B) getting a lot of attention.
    (C) unknown.

All of MSF's international workers are volunteers .

4. *Volunteers* are . . .

    (A) people without specialized training.
    (B) experts.
    (C) people who give their time freely.

One doctor said that practicing medicine at a refugee camp was like getting a hands-on lesson in the history of medicine, far away from his everyday experiences in a modern medical center.

5. A *hands-on* lesson is a . . . lesson.

(A) real-life
(B) painful
(C) free

MSF is best known for its rapid response in times of crisis. When a medical emergency occurs, MSF sends in an advance team to find out what kind of help is needed.

6. Circle the word in these sentences that is closest in meaning to *crisis*.

This team arranges transportation, often to remote areas.

7. *Remote* means . . .

(A) far away.
(B) urban.
(C) mountainous.

In addition, MSF highlights the lack of important drugs in poor nations. MSF points out that fourteen million people die each year from tropical diseases.

8. A phrase in these sentences is close in meaning to *highlights*. Circle this phrase.

In 1999, the Norwegian Nobel Committee awarded MSF the Peace Prize for its "pioneering humanitarian work on several continents."

9. *Humanitarian* work is . . . work.

(A) charitable
(B) essential
(C) difficult

James Orbinski, president of MSF at the time, said that medical aid should be not be tied to wars or politics but only to the dignity of people.

10. *Dignity* is . . .

(A) need.
(B) self-respect.
(C) safety.

While You Read

Here are seven points that appear in the reading passage. There is one point for each paragraph. While you read, put the points in order from 1 to 7.

_____ MSF's Nobel Prize
_____ The growth of MSF
_____ The dangerous work of MSF
_____ The birth and basic beliefs of MSF
_____ The voluntary nature of MSF's work
_____ MSF's educational function
_____ MSF's response in time of crisis

DOCTORS WITHOUT BORDERS

1   In 1971, a small group of doctors in Paris formed an organization. Their goal was to provide emergency medical aid, no matter where it is needed or who needs it. This was the beginning of *Médecins Sans Frontières*, (MSF) or, in English, Doctors Without Borders. The philosophy of MSF is that all people have the right to medical care, regardless of race, religion, or nationality. Today, according to MSF, the world needs medical doctors who can provide aid to any nation quickly, efficiently, and without political pressures.

2   MSF began as "a couple of doctors with a suitcase and a dream." Now it is the largest nongovernmental organization for emergency medical relief. It has offices in twenty countries and has provided medical help in eighty-five countries, including Rwanda, Chechnya, Kosovo, Liberia, Afghanistan, and Iraq. MSF sends teams not only to locations that are in the spotlight but also to places where forgotten wars continue to cause suffering.

3   Because so much of MSF's work is done in dangerous locations, it requires great bravery to be an MSF worker. MSF workers have

been shot at, wounded, kidnapped, and killed. They have also been infected with the diseases that they were trying to fight.

4   All of MSF's international workers are volunteers. Only a small   20 number of the volunteers are doctors. Most volunteers serve as nurses, medical technicians, sanitation engineers, and administrators. Although the volunteers are paid only a small amount to cover their cost of living, they are rewarded in many other ways. One doctor said that practicing medicine at a refugee camp was like getting a hands-   25 on lesson in the history of medicine, far away from his everyday experiences in a modern medical center. Another volunteer summed up her work this way: "It's a life-changing experience."

5   MSF is best known for its rapid response in times of crisis. When a medical emergency occurs, MSF sends in an advance team to find   30 out what kind of help is needed. This team arranges transportation, often to remote areas. Teams may travel by jeep, boat, helicopter, or even on foot. The advance team then contacts one of its four regional centers, located in Europe, East Africa, Central America, and East Asia. The center organizes teams of volunteers and sends   35 kits of supplies and equipment. The membership of the team and the contents of the kits depend on the type of emergency. For example, in a war or natural disaster, MSF sends in medical teams with emergency-room experience and fully equipped surgical tents, electrical generators, medicine, food, and clean water.   40

6   Another important function of MSF is to educate people in developed nations about worldwide medical problems. Every year, the group publishes a list called the Top Ten Underreported Humanitarian Stories about wars and disasters that receive little attention from the international media. MSF also educates people   45 in developing countries about infectious diseases, such as sleeping sickness, malaria, and tuberculosis. In addition, MSF highlights the

Fig. 9.2 The 1999 Nobel Committee awarding the Peace Prize to MSF.

lack of important drugs in poor nations. MSF points out that fourteen million people die each year from tropical diseases. However, out of 1,393 new drugs developed since 1975, only about 1% were targeted at these diseases. 50 55

In 1999, the Norwegian Nobel Committee awarded MSF the Peace Prize[1] for its "pioneering humanitarian work on several continents." This prize is usually given to individuals; only four organizations have received it. James Orbinski, president of MSF at the time, said that medical aid should not be tied to wars or politics, but only to the dignity of people. He went on to say, "An organization like this shows how much can be accomplished with simple and affordable methods." 60

Note

1. In addition to its prizes in fields such as chemistry, economics, and literature, the Nobel Prize Committee awards a *Peace Prize* every year to individuals or organizations that contribute to world peace.

After You Read

⟩ Understanding the Reading

Answer these multiple-choice questions to see how well you understood the reading.

1. Which statement best summarizes the philosophy of MSF?

   (A) Doctors should be able to practice medicine wherever they want.
   (B) People all over the world deserve medical care in emergencies.
   (C) Countries should not have borders so people can travel freely.
   (D) Every nation has the right to manage its own medical services.

2. Which statement about MSF's international workers is true?

   (A) They receive no money to cover daily expenses.
   (B) Almost all of them are doctors.
   (C) Some of them are required to work for MSF by their governments.
   (D) They often have some valuable and unusual experiences.

3. Which is NOT one of the tasks of an advance MSF team?

   (A) To arrange transportation for MSF workers
   (B) To determine what kind of aid is required
   (C) To communicate with an MSF regional center
   (D) To set up surgical tents and electrical generators

4. How many regional centers does MSF have?

   (A) Four
   (B) Ten
   (C) Twenty
   (D) Eighty-five

5. What do the contents of the kits of medical supplies and equipment mainly depend on?

   (A) The kind of emergency
   (B) The number of people in the team
   (C) The location of the emergency
   (D) The cost of supplies and equipment

6. What list does MSF publish every year?

   (A) The ten most terrible disasters
   (B) The ten worst infectious diseases
   (C) Ten disasters or wars that received little international attention
   (D) Ten ways to help the MSF do its work

7. Since 1975, how many drugs have been developed to treat tropical infectious diseases?

   (A) Only one
   (B) About fourteen
   (C) About thirty
   (D) 1,393

8. Who usually receives Nobel Peace Prizes?

(A) Government organizations
(B) National governments
(C) Private international organizations
(D) Individuals

≫ Vocabulary Building

Fill in the blanks in the sentences below with one of these words or phrases from the reading.

efficiently	sanitation	kit	media	hands-on
regardless	kidnapped	summed up	highlights	pioneering
pressures	volunteers	remote	targeted	humanitarian

1. The E-Institute offers _____ training for people interested in designing Web pages. Each student has to create his or her own personal Web site.

2. When I was a child, my uncle once took me swimming without telling my mother. My mother thought someone had _____ me.

3. Like MSF, the International Red Cross/Red Crescent is a _____ organization.

4. A: A button came off my shirt.

   B: There's a sewing _____ in your hotel room. It has needles, thread, and a small pair of scissors in it.

5. I like to get my news from a variety of _____: newspapers, magazines, radio, and television.

6. Antismoking activists were angry when a tobacco company used cartoon characters to advertise cigarettes. The activists said that these advertisements were _____ at children.

7. Some nations require citizens to serve in the military. Other countries depend on _____.

8. Nikola Tesla was an innovator in the field of electronics and made many _____ discoveries.

Reading Skill: Scanning

In Unit 4, you practiced skimming. Skimming is a kind of speed reading. It is reading quickly to get the main idea or to get general information from a text. Scanning is another speed-reading skill. However, scanning is reading quickly to find short answers to specific questions.

Scanning is useful for finding facts, rather than ideas. It is an easier skill to master than skimming. Names, numbers, dates, and other such facts "stand out" in a reading and are usually easy to find. First, however, you must know what to look for. You always look for key terms in the question being asked, but you must also look for synonyms and related terms. Then your eyes search the text quickly for the terms.

Example

Question: When was MSF founded?

Key terms: founded, MSF, and dates (to answer "when")

Synonyms and Related Terms: formed, began, started

To quickly find the answer to the question, scan the reading for the key words. The answer is located in paragraph one, in the first sentence. The synonym "formed" is used instead of *founded*. The correct answer is 1971.

Exercise: Scan the reading quickly to find the answers to the questions, and write your answers in the blanks. Remember: speed is important! Work as fast as you can. Clock your time in the spaces provided, and try to finish the entire exercise in less than three minutes.

Beginning time: _____

1. How many new drugs have been developed since 1975?

   _____

2. Who was president of MSF in 1999? _____

3. Worldwide, how many people die each year of tropical diseases?

   _____

4. MSF volunteers serve in what jobs? Give one example besides doctors.

   _____

5. What do MSF volunteers receive money for?

   _____

6. What is an example of an infectious disease that MSF educates people about? _____

7. Where was MSF founded? _____

8. How many "Underreported Humanitarian Stories" does the MSF report every year? _____

Ending time: _____

⟫ Focus on Listening

Listen to the recording of the reading "Doctors Without Borders." You will hear this reading two times. The first time, read along with the recording and focus on the speaker's pronunciation and intonation. The second time, listen for meaning. Do not look at the reading. Try to follow the ideas by listening only.

As you listen the second time, the speaker will stop occasionally and make statements about the reading. Decide if the statements are true or false. Fill in the space of the circled T or F according to what you hear and remember from the reading.

1. Ⓣ Ⓕ   5. Ⓣ Ⓕ
2. Ⓣ Ⓕ   6. Ⓣ Ⓕ
3. Ⓣ Ⓕ   7. Ⓣ Ⓕ
4. Ⓣ Ⓕ   8. Ⓣ Ⓕ

⟫ Writing and Discussion Questions

Work with a partner or group to complete these questions.

1. Using the Internet, research other organizations like MSF. Get some facts on two or three listed here. Find out when each organization was founded, where its headquarters is located, what kind of work it does, and any other interesting facts. Write several sentences about each organization that you choose.

Doctor to Doctor	Project Hope
Healing Hands International	Ashinaga
The International Red Cross/Red Crescent	Oxfam
Engineers Without Borders	Carter Center
International Rescue Committee	Action Against Hunger
Refugees International	CARE International

2. Using the Internet, find information about three winners of the Nobel Peace Prize and scan for biographical facts. Exchange facts with your classmates.

3. Imagine that you are going to spend the next year of your life as a volunteer for an international agency. What kind of work would you like to do? What country would you like to work in? Give reasons for your choices.

⧫ Crossword Puzzle

Complete the puzzle with words from the reading.

Across

1 Help; aid
3 Tropical disease
5 Doctors Without Borders initials
6 _____ Peace Prize
9 People who work willingly and without pay
10 Emergency; disaster

Down

1 Far away; isolated
2 Cost of _____
4 People who must leave their own countries
7 _____-on training
8 City where Doctors Without Borders began

Sister Act: Venus and Serena Williams

Fig. 10.1

Before You Read

» Warm-Up Questions

Discuss these questions in pairs or groups. Share your ideas with the class.

1. Do you recognize the women in the photograph? What sport are they playing? How do you know?

2. How old are Venus and Serena? Where are they from? Scan the reading for some facts about the Williams sisters.

3. This reading is a biography. It tells you about the Williams sisters' life. What other reading in this book is a biography? Whose life does it discuss?

❱ Vocabulary Preview

These statements come from the reading "Sister Act: Venus and Serena Williams."
Read each statement and then answer the questions that follow. Check your
answers before you begin the reading.

Fascinated , Richard saw Virginia Ruzici win the match and receive a $220,000 prize.

1. This sentence tells us that Richard was very . . . the match.

   (A) nervous about
   (B) emotional about
   (C) interested in

When the sisters were still very young, Richard loaded used tennis rackets and
boxes full of battered tennis balls into his old Volkswagen . . .

2. If tennis balls are *battered,* they are . . .

   (A) worn and in poor condition.
   (B) brand new.
   (C) inexpensive.

"Venus and Serena took to tennis as soon as rackets were put in their hands."

3. Venus and Serena . . . tennis.

   (A) showed a natural talent for
   (B) wanted to stop playing
   (C) were forced to play

In 1990, the *New York Times* published a series of articles about promising young
people. The headline of the article about Venus read: "Status: Undefeated. Future:
Rosy . Age: 10."

4. Circle another word that means *rosy.*

However, their father withdrew them from tournaments so that they could focus on
school.

5. In other words, their father . . . tournaments.

   (A) encouraged them to play in
   (B) took them out of
   (C) trained them to play in

The sisters went from one triumph to another

6. A *triumph* is a . . .

   (A) tournament.
   (B) lesson.
   (C) success.

In 2001, they became the first siblings to compete against each other in the finals at Wimbledon since Maud Watson played Lillian Watson in 1884.

7. *Siblings* are . . .

   (A) amateurs.
   (B) brothers or sisters.
   (C) first-time winners.

Fans admire their confidence, intelligence, and sense of style. They studied fashion at the Florida Art Institute, and they design their own eye-catching tennis clothes.

8. Circle the word that is closest in meaning to *fashion*.

They have endorsed tennis shoes, chewing gum, milk, and toys.

9. In other words, they . . . these products.

   (A) spoke in favor of
   (B) refused to buy
   (C) won

"This is unheard of . It's never happened in tennis, and I don't think it has happened in sports . . ."

10. The phrase *unheard of* means . . . .

   (A) unsurprising.
   (B) unforgettable.
   (C) unknown.

While You Read

Here are nine points that appear in the reading passage. There is one point for each paragraph. While you read, put the points in order from 1 to 9.

_____ The sisters' early successes and their father's prediction
_____ The second stage of the sisters' training
_____ Success for the Williams sisters outside of tennis
_____ Why the sisters are unique in sports
_____ Reasons for the sisters' success in tennis
_____ The origin of Richard Williams' interest in tennis
_____ The sisters' victories as professionals
_____ Venus and Serena's earliest training
_____ The move to Florida

SISTER ACT: VENUS AND SERENA WILLIAMS

1   In June, 1978, Richard Williams and his wife Oracene watched
the French Open[1] in their home in southern California. Fascinated,
Richard saw Virginia Ruzici win the match and receive a $220,000
prize. That day, Richard, father of three daughters, told Oracene, "If
we have more children, I'll teach them to play tennis."   5

2   Venus Williams was born in 1980, and her sister Serena was born
a year and a half later. Their father read books and watched videos
to learn tennis skills. When the sisters were still very young, Richard
loaded used tennis rackets and boxes full of battered tennis balls into
his old Volkswagen, drove to a tennis court, and began teaching   10
them to play. According to older sister Lyndrea, "Venus and Serena
took to tennis as soon as rackets were put in their hands." While the
girls played, Richard sat on the sideline shouting instructions from
tennis books. The tennis courts where they practiced were in
Compton, a poor suburb of Los Angeles known for its high crime   15
rate. The courts were in terrible condition, and there was not even a
net until Richard complained. Then a heavy metal net was installed.
Whenever a ball hit the net, Richard thought it was a gunshot.

3   In 1988, the girls trained with tennis pro[2] Paul Cohen in
Brentwood, a wealthy section of Los Angeles. Tennis star Pete   20

Sampras saw the girls play there, and Sampras even hit a few balls with Venus. Afterwards, Venus told her father, "If we had played a real game, I could have beaten him."

4   The girls began playing in the junior tennis association, and soon they were both number one in their age divisions. In 1990, the *New* 25 *York Times*[3] published a series of articles about promising young people. The headline of the article about Venus read: "Status: Undefeated. Future: Rosy. Age: 10." Richard began to tell people that, someday, his girls would be the best women players in the world. Some people thought Richard was too much of a "tennis dad."[4] They 30 believed he forced his daughters to be too competitive and made them practice too much. In reality, if he thought the girls concentrated too much on tennis, he sent them to a shopping mall or to the beach.

5   In 1991, the Williams family moved to Florida, and Venus and Serena attended the Delray Beach Tennis Academy. For the next four 35 years, the girls practiced with coach Rick Macci six hours a day, seven days a week. However, their father withdrew them from tournaments so that they could focus on school. They went to Driftwood Academy, a small, private high school. Both graduated as top students.

6   At fourteen, Venus became a professional, and Serena soon 40 joined her. In a few years, they were playing in important tournaments. Serena was the first of the two to win a Grand Slam[5] event, defeating Martina Hingis in the U.S. Open in 1999. The sisters went from one triumph to another. In 2000, Venus won singles[6] titles at both Wimbledon and the U.S. Open and the gold 45 medal for singles at the Sydney Olympics. She and her sister won the gold medal for doubles[7] in Sydney. In 2001, they became the first siblings to compete against each other in the finals at Wimbledon since Maud Watson played Lillian Watson in 1884, a game played in long skirts and fancy hats. The Williams sisters 50

continued to win doubles tournaments and to face each other in singles championships, most of which Serena won. Their father's dream of their becoming champions had come true.

7   Why have the Williams sisters been so successful? Observers say that it's because of their early training, their tough mental attitude, and their physical strength. They both have powerful serves and returns.[8] Their serves travel more than 200 kilometers per hour.

8   The sisters have succeeded off the court as well. Fans admire their confidence, intelligence, and sense of style. They studied fashion at the Florida Art Institute, and they design their own eye-catching tennis clothes. They have endorsed tennis shoes, chewing gum, milk, and toys. They are smart businesswomen and are on lists of the world's richest women. They have appeared in music videos and on television shows.

9   As African-Americans from a poor family, the Williams sisters are a rarity in professional tennis, a sport generally dominated by white, wealthy people. Not since 1975, when Arthur Ashe won at Wimbledon, has a black player done so well. And not since 1957, when Althea Gibson won the U.S. Open and Wimbledon, has a black woman been so successful. Because of their superstar status, they are most often compared with golfer Tiger Woods, another minority player in a sport usually dominated by players from wealthy families. Like Tiger, the Williams sisters were driven by an ambitious father and began playing before kindergarten. Like him, they have brought a new audience to their sport and have donated their time to train young players. However, as a "sister act,"[9] Venus and Serena are unique. Tennis star and commentator John McEnroe said, "This is unheard of. It's never happened in tennis, and I don't think it has happened in sports, where the number one and two face off against each other, and yet still love each other so much."

Notes

1. *The French Open* is one of the most important tournaments in professional tennis.

2. *Tennis pro* is short for "tennis professional." Tennis pros make their living from tennis. They may compete in tournaments or teach tennis classes.

3. The *New York Times* is one of the top daily newspapers in the United States.

4. A *tennis dad* is the father of a child or children who play tennis. Tennis dads (and moms) cheer their children on and often try to make them play harder. There are also soccer dads, skating moms, and so on.

5. *The Grand Slam tournaments* are the four most important tennis tournaments that are played every year: Wimbledon (played in the U.K.), the U.S. Open, the French Open, and the Australian Open.

6. *Singles* means that one player competes against another player.

7. *Doubles* means that two players compete against two other players.

8. A *serve* is when a tennis player hits a ball to begin play. A *return* is when a player hits a ball to the other side of the court. A player can returen either a serve or another return.

9. The term *sister act* usually refers to two or more sisters who perform together as entertainers: singers, comedians, etc.

After You Read

⟫ Understanding the Reading

Answer these multiple-choice questions to see how well you understood the reading.

1. Which of these events made Richard Williams want his daughters to become tennis players?

   (A) He saw the French Open on television.
   (B) He won a tennis championship himself as a young man.
   (C) He and his wife attended a tennis match while in France.
   (D) He read a fascinating book about tennis.

2. How many older sisters does Serena Williams have?

   (A) One
   (B) Two
   (C) Three
   (D) Four

3. What does the reference to the gunshot at the end of paragraph 2 tell you?

   (A) How far the girls hit the ball
   (B) How strong the metal net was
   (C) How loud Richard had to shout
   (D) How dangerous the neighborhood was

4. According to the reading, which statement about tennis star Pete Sampras is true?

   (A) He spent many months training the Williams sisters.
   (B) Venus defeated him in a real game.
   (C) Venus believed that she could win in a game against him.
   (D) He came to Compton to watch the sisters practice.

5. Richard Williams withdrew his girls from tournaments because he . . .

   (A) didn't think they were ready to compete.
   (B) wanted them to focus on their high school studies.
   (C) thought the sisters were becoming too competitive.
   (D) thought the sisters were winning too easily.

6. What did the Williams sisters probably study at the Florida Art Institute?

   (A) Clothing design
   (B) Art history
   (C) Advertising
   (D) Movie making

7. The Williams sisters are most frequently compared to . . .

   (A) Maud and Lillian Watson.
   (B) Arthur Ashe.
   (C) Althea Gibson.
   (D) Tiger Woods.

8. John McEnroe says that what the Williams sisters have done has never happened before in sports. He probably would not say this if which of the following statements were true?

(A) Venus and Serena played golf, not tennis.
(B) The Williams sisters came from a wealthy family.
(C) Tiger Woods had a beloved brother who was also a champion golfer.
(D) Althea Gibson was still playing tennis.

❯ Vocabulary Building

Fill in the blanks in the sentences below with one of these words or phrases from the reading.

loaded	complained	withdrew	endorsed	ambitious
battered	shout	titles	eye-catching	unheard of
terrible	rosy	siblings	rarity	face off
installed	concentrated	fancy	dominated	drove to

1. Our team and Fairview University both won the semifinals games. Now we'll _____ in the finals.

2. A: My neighbors play loud music when I'm trying to sleep.

   B: Have you said anything to them?

   A: Yes, I've _____ several times, but it hasn't done any good.

3. The president predicted a _____ future for the country, but economic conditions haven't gotten better.

4. NBA basketball star Yao Ming has _____ several products in television commercials, including computers and credit cards.

5. Thomas is a very _____ actor. He plans to win an Academy Award within five years.

6. Johanna's car looks old and _____, but its engine is still in good condition.

7. The workers _____ the equipment onto the truck.

8. It was so noisy in the nightclub that I had to _____ to make my friends hear me.

Reading Skill: Understanding Conditional Sentences

This reading has several conditional sentences. A conditional sentence contains the word *if* and has two clauses: the *if* clause and the main clause.

If clause	Main clause
If you score the next point,	you will win the game.

Conditionals can be difficult for readers. They state that one thing depends on another thing. To understand a conditional sentence you must know what type of conditional it is and understand the verbs in both clauses.

1A. Present Factual

If you throw a ball against a wall, it bounces.

This type of sentence really means: "Whenever A happens, B always happens."

1B. Past Factual

Last year, if I practiced every day, my tennis game improved.

This type of sentence means: "In the past, whenever A happened, B always happened."

2. Predictive

If it rains, we'll play on the indoor court.

This type of sentence means: "Perhaps A will happen. If it does, B will (or might, or can) happen."

3A. Present Contrary to Fact

If I had a better serve, I would win more games.

This type of sentence means: "A is not true; but if, in fact, A were true, B would (or could, or might) happen."

3B. Past Contrary to Fact

If John had been my partner, we would have won the game.

This type of sentence means: "A did not happen; but if, in fact, A had happened, B would have (or could have, or might have) happened."

Exercise: First, decide which type of conditional each sentence is. Mark the sentences 1A, 1B, 2, 3A, or 3B) according to the explanations above. Then decide if the second statement is true or false based on the conditional sentence.

Example

_3A_ If I were in France, I would go to the French Open.
I am going to the French Open. (T) **(F)**

____ 1. Richard Williams told his wife, "If we have more children, I'll teach them to play tennis."
Richard was not sure that they would have more children. (T) (F)

____ 2. If a ball hit the heavy metal net, it sounded like a gunshot.
The balls never hit the net. (T) (F)

____ 3. If Richard had not complained, the city would not have installed a net.
The city did not install a net. (T) (F)

____ 4. If Serena plays her sister Venus in a singles match, Serena usually wins.
Venus usually loses in singles matches against her sister Serena. (T) (F)

____ 5. If Richard thought the girls concentrated too much on tennis, he sent them to a shopping mall or to the beach.
Sometimes the girls concentrated on tennis too much, and then Richard sent them to the beach or a mall. (T) (F)

____ 6. If the Watson sisters still played tennis, they could play doubles against the Williams sisters.
The Watson sisters no longer play tennis. (T) (F)

____ 7. If the Williams sisters were from a wealthy family, their success in tennis might not be considered such a rarity.
The Williams sisters came from a wealthy family. (T) (F)

____ 8. If someone makes a movie about Venus and Serena's lives, it will probably be a big success.
Someone has made a movie about the lives of Venus and Serena. (T) (F)

➤ Focus on Listening

Listen to the recording of the reading "Sister Act: Venus and Serena Williams." You will hear this reading two times. The first time, read along with the recording and focus on the speaker's pronunciation and intonation. The second time, listen for meaning. Do not look at the reading. Try to follow the ideas by listening only.

As you listen the second time, the speaker will stop occasionally and make statements about the reading. Decide if the statements are true or false. Fill in the space of the circled T or F according to what you hear and remember from the reading.

1. Ⓣ Ⓕ   5. Ⓣ Ⓕ

2. Ⓣ Ⓕ   6. Ⓣ Ⓕ

3. Ⓣ Ⓕ   7. Ⓣ Ⓕ

4. Ⓣ Ⓕ   8. Ⓣ Ⓕ

➤ Writing and Discussion Questions

Work with a partner or group to complete these questions.

1. Using the Internet, get some basic biographical information about a sports star you are interested in.

2. Using the Internet or a dictionary, find the meaning of as many of these tennis terms as possible and write definitions.

love	match	point	lob
forehand	out of bounds	deuce	smash
backhand	racquet	set	sweet spot

3. If a young child shows a lot of promise in some sport such as tennis, swimming, or golf, do you think that child's parents should push the child to be successful and to practice continuously? Explain your reasons.

4. If you could be superstar in any sport, which sport would you choose? Why?

5. If you could be successful in sports, art, music, movies, or business, which field would you choose? Why?

❯ Crossword Puzzle

Complete the puzzle with words from the reading.

Across

1 Optimistic; promising

4 Tennis star Arthur _____

6 Older of the two tennis-playing Williams sisters

8 To _____ off with is to compete against

9 Championships

10 Objected; protested

11 Maud and Lillian _____

Down

2 Younger of the two tennis-playing Williams sisters

3 _____ Woods, golf superstar

5 Spoke in favor of

7 Sisters or brothers

8 Ornamental; elaborate

Hurray for Bollywood!

Fig. 11.1

Before You Read

Warm-Up Questions

Discuss these questions in pairs or groups. Share your ideas with the class.

1. Why do you go to movies? To be entertained? To learn? To escape your problems? Explain your answer.

2. Describe the photo on this page. What kind of movie is this photo from?

3. Have you ever heard of Bollywood? Look over the reading for some facts about the cinema of India.

▶ Vocabulary Preview

These statements come from the reading "Hurray for Bollywood!" Read each statement and then answer the questions that follow. Check your answers before you begin the reading.

Like most early Indian movies, it is about religion and mythology .

1. *Mythology* is . . .

(A) history.
(B) stories of gods and goddesses.
(C) philosophy.

It was virtually impossible for an Indian actor or actress to be successful without the ability to sing and dance.

2. If something is *virtually* impossible, it is . . . impossible.

(A) completely
(B) almost
(C) temporarily

Indian movies of this time were mostly sentimental musical extravaganzas . . . . Typical Bollywood musicals tend to follow very strict formulas .

3. *Extravaganzas* are . . . .

(A) spectacular shows.
(B) inexpensive productions.
(C) tragic love stories.

4. Movies that follow *strict formulas* . . .

(A) are carefully controlled by the government.
(B) need a lot of planning.
(C) use similar stories again and again.

They are romantic and lighthearted , and they feature glamorous costumes .

5. If something is *lighthearted* it is . . .

(A) not exciting.
(B) heartbreaking.
(C) not serious.

6. What are *glamorous costumes?*

(A) Attractive clothing
(B) Beautiful scenery
(C) Love stories

Actors suddenly begin to sing and dance for no apparent reason , and the songs are often unrelated to the story.

7. If something happens *for no apparent reason . . .*

(A) it's easy to understand why it happens.
(B) it doesn't really happen, it just seems to happen.
(C) it's not clear why it happens.

Bollywood movies provide an escape for their audiences, but they are sometimes criticized for being too formulaic and lacking substance .

8. If something is *lacking substance,* it is . . .

(A) not concerned with serious issues.
(B) as realistic as possible.
(C) not very creative.

From the beginning, India has loved its stars. Bollywood actors and actresses are even more adored than Hollywood performers.

9. Circle the word that is closest in meaning to *adored.*

Because stars attract audiences to movies, studios have raised their salaries to incredible levels.

10. A synonym for *incredible* is . . .

(A) unrewarding.
(B) uninteresting.
(C) unbelievable.

While You Read

Here are six points that appear in the reading passage. There is one point for each paragraph. While you read, put the points in order from 1 to 6.

_____ Early Bollywood movies
_____ Bollywood's growing influence abroad
_____ Bollywood movies from the 1950s to the present
_____ The success of two Bollywood movies outside of India
_____ The size of the Bollywood film industry
_____ Bollywood stars

HURRAY FOR BOLLYWOOD!

1   What city makes more movies than any other city in the world?   1
If you said Hollywood, sorry, you're wrong. The correct answer is
Bombay.[1] The Indian film industry has been nicknamed Bollywood,
a combination of the words *Bombay* and *Hollywood*. Bollywood
makes around one thousand films a year, while Hollywood makes   5
only about seven hundred. Cinema is a major industry in India. There
are over thirteen thousand movie theaters in India, and everyday
about fifteen million people go to the movies. Bollywood films are
also popular in other countries, especially in cities with large Indian
populations, such as London, Toronto, and San Francisco.   10

2   As elsewhere, Indian cinema began with silent movies.
Ramayana[2] (1917) was the first. It was directed by D. G. Phalke,
the father of Indian cinema. Like most early Indian movies, it is
about religion and mythology. *Alam Ara* (1931) was the first
Bollywood "talkie." Talkies soon replaced silent movies, and music   15
and dance quickly became an important part of Indian cinema.
Some movies, such as *Sabha* (1932), consisted of nothing but
musical numbers. *Sabha* contained a record seventy-two songs. It
was virtually impossible for an Indian actor or actress to be
successful without the ability to sing and dance.   20

3   The "Golden Age" of Bollywood was the 1950s and 60s. Indian movies of this time were mostly sentimental musical extravaganzas. During the 1970s, Bollywood studios changed to action films. However, in the 1980s, they returned to music and romance. Typical Bollywood musicals tend to follow very strict formulas. The most common formula is: "Rich boy meets poor girl, and after many complications, they marry." These movies are long, usually three hours or more. They are romantic and lighthearted, and they feature glamorous costumes. Actors suddenly begin to sing and dance for no apparent reason, and the songs are often unrelated to the story. Song and dance scenes suddenly shift to faraway locations: a beach in the Maldives,[3] a street in Scotland, a forest in New Zealand, or a mountain meadow in Switzerland. These movies often end with joyful wedding scenes. Bollywood movies provide an escape for their audiences, but they are sometimes criticized for being too formulaic and lacking substance.

4   In recent years, a number of more serious Indian movies have been made, and some have been successful internationally. *Lagaan* (2001) is about a cricket[4] match in the nineteenth century between Indian villagers and British colonial soldiers. The movie criticizes colonialism, but it has a comic tone. *Monsoon Wedding* (2001), like many Indian movies, deals with love, marriage, and family. However, this film is much more realistic than most Indian films about weddings.

5   From the beginning, India has loved its stars. Bollywood actors and actresses are even more adored than Hollywood performers. In one poll, Amitabh Bachchan, India's greatest superstar, was voted more popular than national heroes

Fig. 11.2 Amitabh Bachchan.

such as Gandhi and Nehru. The current generation of stars, which includes Madhuri Dixit, Juhi Chawla, and Salman Khan, is just as popular. Because stars attract audiences to movies, studios have raised their salaries to incredible levels. Bollywood films are expensive to make, and the high salaries are the main reason why.   55

6   Bollywood's influence continues to grow internationally. A play about Bollywood, *Bombay Dreams*, is a hit in London. In the big Hollywood movie *Moulin Rouge* (2001), actress Nicole Kidman borrows the "Chamma-Chamma" song from the Bollywood movie   60 *China Gate* (2000). Concerts featuring Bollywood music are sold out in China, and Bollywood clothing fashions are seen on models in Europe. Bollywood has gone from a national phenomenon to a global one.

Notes

1. *Bombay*—also known as Mombai—is one of the largest cities in India.
2. The *Ramayana* is a long, very old poem about Hindu gods and goddesses.
3. The *Maldives* are a group of islands in the Indian Ocean.
4. *Cricket* is a popular team sport played in the U.K., India, New Zealand, Australia, South Africa, and other countries.

After You Read

❯ Understanding the Reading

Answer these multiple-choice questions to see how well you understood the reading.

1. How many movies are made by Bollywood every year?

   (A) Seven hundred
   (B) One thousand
   (C) One thousand five hundred
   (D) Thirteen thousand

2. Which statement about *Sabha* is true?

   (A) It was a silent movie.
   (B) It was the first Indian "talkie."
   (C) It only had songs and dances.
   (D) It was about religion and mythology.

3. When did Bollywood make a lot of action movies?

   (A) In the 1950s and 1960s
   (B) In the 1970s
   (C) In the 1980s
   (D) In the 1990s

4. Which of these is NOT a characteristic of typical Bollywood movies?

   (A) They usually last three hours or more.
   (B) The songs and dances are often unrelated to the story.
   (C) They usually end in unhappy ways.
   (D) The musical scenes may take place all over the world.

5. Which best describes the movie *Lagaan*?

   (A) The story of the best cricket team playing in India today
   (B) The happy story of an Indian wedding
   (C) The sad story of a battle between villagers and colonial soldiers
   (D) The story of a cricket game in colonial India

6. The reading mentions a poll in paragraph 5. Which of these questions was probably asked in the poll?

   (A) Who is your favorite movie star in the world?
   (B) Which of these famous Indians do you like the most?
   (C) What is your favorite movie?
   (D) Who is the greatest Indian politician?

7. Which of these is the main reason for the high production costs of Bollywood movies?

   (A) The high salaries of Indian movie stars
   (B) The expensive costumes required for musical scenes
   (C) The costs of filming scenes all over the world
   (D) The length of most Bollywood movies

8. What does the author say about the movie star Nicole Kidman?

(A) She was in a Bollywood movie.
(B) She was in a play about Bollywood.
(C) She sang a song from a Bollywood movie.
(D) She wears Bollywood fashions.

» Vocabulary Building

Fill in the blanks in the sentences below with one of these words or phrases from the reading.

combination	extravaganzas	phenomenon	apparent	current
mythology	strict	glamorous	adored	influence
virtually	tend to	costumes	deals with	sentimental
lighthearted	formulas	shift	poll	far away

1. My grandfather _____ literature. He read all of the classics over and over.

2. A moped is a type of motorbike. The word *moped* is a _____ of the words *motor* and *pedal*.

3. According to a recent _____, more people in this city are concerned about crime than any other problem.

4. Professor McClure is a tough teacher with a _____ grading policy, but you'll learn a lot if you take her class.

5. Mr. Suzuki was the _____ winner of the election, but when the votes were re-counted Ms. Olson was the real winner.

6. In the 1930s, Hollywood made many musical _____ with hundreds of dancers and singers and elaborate musical scenes.

7. I would love to be a fashion photographer. I think that would be such a _____ job.

8. In the 1970s, the television show "All in the Family" was very popular even though it didn't follow any of the typical _____ for American television comedies.

Reading Skill: Paraphrasing

When you *paraphrase*, you write someone else's ideas in your own words. That is, you rewrite the idea. Paraphrasing is a useful skill for many reasons. You may need to paraphrase if you are summarizing an article, a book, or doing research of any kind. Recognizing paraphrases is also important for standardized tests. Last, it is an excellent way to help you understand a difficult idea.

There are a several ways you can paraphrase material.

1. Use synonyms for some of the words in the original

2. Rearrange the parts of the sentences

3. Use different grammatical structures from the ones in the original

Be sure to read the material BEFORE you attempt to rewrite it. Don't look back at the passage as you rewrite.

Example:

India is currently responsible for about a fourth of all the movies made in the world.

Today, about a quarter of the world's films are produced in India.

The two sentences use different vocabulary, grammar, and word order, but they have about the same meaning.

Exercise 1: Here are six sentences based on information in the reading. Mark the second sentence **P** if it correctly paraphrases the first sentence. Mark it **X** if it does not.

1. Bollywood films are also popular in other countries, especially in cities with large Indian populations such as London, Toronto, and San Francisco.

    _____ Indian immigrants in cities such as London, Toronto, and San Francisco enjoy Bollywood movies even more than audiences in India.

2. It was virtually impossible for an Indian actor or actress to be successful without the ability to sing and dance.

    _____ To do well, Indian actors and actresses were practically required to have singing and dancing skills.

3. Bollywood movies of this time were mostly sentimental musical

extravaganzas. . . . Typical Bollywood musicals tend to follow very strict formulas.

_____ Most Bollywood films are spectacular musicals with similar structures and stories.

4. *Monsoon Wedding* (2001), like many Indian movies, deals with love, marriage, and family. However, this film is much more realistic than most Indian films about weddings.

_____ *Monsoon Wedding* is not as realistic as most Indian films, and it is about a subject that Indian films almost never deal with.

5. In one poll, Amitabh Bachchan, India's greatest superstar, was voted more popular than national heroes such as Gandhi and Nehru.

_____ National figures—for example, Gandhi and Nehru—were liked more than movie stars—for instance, Amitabh Bachchan— according to one poll.

6. Because stars attract audiences to movies, studios have raised their salaries to incredible levels. Bollywood movies are expensive to make and the inflated salaries are the main reason why.

_____ The cost of making Bollywood movies is quite high. The most important reason for this is the unbelievable salaries paid to Bollywood movie stars.

Exercise 2: Paraphrase these sentences from the reading.

1. Bollywood makes around one thousand films a year, while Hollywood makes only about seven hundred.

   _____

   _____

2. Actors suddenly begin to sing and dance for no apparent reason, and the songs are often unrelated to the story.

   _____

   _____

3. Bollywood movies provide an escape for their audiences, but they are sometimes criticized for being formulistic and lacking substance.

   _____

   _____

4. Concerts featuring Bollywood music are sold out in China, and Bollywood

clothing fashions are seen on models in Europe.

_____

_____

» Focus on Listening

Listen to the recording of the reading "Hurray for Bollywood!" You will hear this reading two times. The first time, read along with the recording and focus on the speaker's pronunciation and intonation. The second time, listen for meaning. Do not look at the reading. Try to follow the ideas by listening only.

As you listen the second time, the speaker will stop occasionally and make statements about the reading. Decide if the statements are true or false. Fill in the space of the circled T or F according to what you hear and remember from the reading.

1. (T) (F)   5. (T) (F)

2. (T) (F)   6. (T) (F)

3. (T) (F)   7. (T) (F)

4. (T) (F)   8. (T) (F)

» Writing and Discussion Questions

Work with a partner or group to complete these questions.

1. Research the history of any country's cinema. Then write a short (one-to-two-paragraph) report about it.

2. Using the Internet, find out about one movie and one star from the list below. If possible, get photos too. Write several sentences about the movie and star that you choose. Exchange your Bollywood facts with classmates.

Movies

Pather Panchali (1955)   *China Gate* (1998)

Mother India (1957)   *Monsoon Wedding* (2001)

Jewel Thief (1967)   *Devdas* (2002)

Sholay (1975)   *Bhoot* (2003)

Movie stars

Amitabh Bachchan	Salman Khan	Vivek Oberoi
Juhi Chawla	Shahrukh Khan	Asha Parek
Sunny Deol	Akshay Kumar	Gracie Singh
Madhuri Dixit	Ashok Kumar	Sridevi
Kareena Kapoor	Dilip Kumar	Mary Evans Wadia

3. Tell a partner about your favorite movie, giving as much detail as possible. Then, when your partner tells you about his or her favorite movie, take notes. Afterwards, briefly tell the class about your partner's favorite movie.

❯ Crossword Puzzle

Complete the puzzle with words from the reading.

Across

1 Movie with seventy-two songs

6 Present; modern

7 Father of Indian cinema, D. G. _____

8 Stories of gods, goddesses, and heroes

9 Change; move

Down

2 Loved; worshiped

3 Bollywood superstar, _____ Bachchan

4 Almost; practically

5 Emotional

6 Clothing, especially when worn by actors and actresses

7 A study; a survey

Krakatoa, West of Java

Fig. 12.1 1883 Drawing of Krakatoa in 1883.

Before You Read

Warm-Up Questions

Discuss these questions in pairs or groups. Share your ideas with the class.

1. What is happening in the picture on this page? Look at the title and skim the first paragraph of the reading. Where is Krakatoa? What happened there?

2. What kinds of natural disasters happen where you live? Have you or anyone you know ever lived through one? Tell the class about the experience.

❯ Vocabulary Preview

These statements come from the reading "Krakatoa, West of Java." Read each statement and then answer the questions that follow. Check your answers before you begin the reading.

The movie *Krakatoa, East of Java* (1969) was about the eruption of a volcano, Krakatoa, in 1883. It was filled with inaccurate information.

1. *Inaccurate* information is . . .

    (A) incorrect.
    (B) useful.
    (C) possibly true, possibly false.

The earth shook and rumbled , smoke and ash poured into the air.

2. Which of these *rumble*?

    (A) Thunderstorms
    (B) Housecats
    (C) Telephones

On August 26, at about 1 P.M., the first of four mighty explosions occurred. Smoke rose 27 kilometers into the air. Three more blasts, each more powerful than the last, followed the next day.

3. Find and circle another word that means *mighty*.

The walls of the volcanic cone collapsed , and seawater poured into the lava chamber below the volcano, turning into superheated steam.

4. The walls *collapsed* means that they . . .

    (A) were blown into the air.
    (B) were stronger than the explosion.
    (C) fell down.

The waves swept over a penal settlement on Enggano Island, killing all the prisoners.

5. A *penal settlement* is a . . .

    (A) resort island.
    (B) prison colony.
    (C) fishing village.

Thirty-kilogram boulders fell on islands 100 kilometers away.

6. *Boulders* are . . .

(A) pieces of burning wood.
(B) small ships.
(C) big rocks.

These pumice rafts washed up on beaches in Africa and South Pacific islands years later, sometimes with tree roots, animal skeletons, and even human remains aboard them.

7. Circle the word that is closest in meaning to *remains* in this selection.

The fine ash traveled around the world and spread to the northern latitudes.

8. In this sentence, *fine* means that the ash . . .

(A) was very useful and beneficial for people.
(B) consisted of very small particles.
(C) was still hot.

The remaining islands were lifeless, burned by fire and buried in ash. Therefore, they could serve as laboratories for biologists who wanted to study how life develops in a sterile environment.

9. Circle another word that means *sterile*.

While You Read

Here are nine points that appear in the reading passage. There is one point for each paragraph. While you read, put the points in order from 1 to 9.

_____ The waking of Krakatoa
_____ The eruption produces giant, destructive waves
_____ Biological "laboratories" on the remnants of Krakatoa
_____ An inaccurate movie and a terrible disaster
_____ Global cooling, a result of the Krakatoa eruption
_____ The first great global news story
_____ The birth of "Krakatoa's child"
_____ The effect of rock and ash blown into the air
_____ The four great explosions

KRAKATOA, WEST OF JAVA

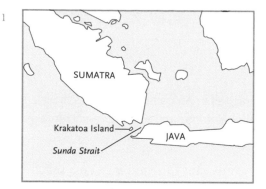

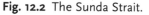

Fig. 12.2 The Sunda Strait.

The movie *Krakatoa, East of Java* (1969) was about the eruption of a volcano, Krakatoa, in 1883. It was filled with inaccurate information. The most inaccurate thing about it was its title: Krakatoa is in the Sunda Strait, south of Sumatra and *west*, not east, of Java. The movie involved hidden treasure, hot air balloons, and pirates, but the actual event was not an exciting adventure. In fact, the eruption was one of history's worst natural disasters. Today, on the Javanese coast 40 kilometers from Krakatoa, tourists relax on Carita Beach. The Indonesian word *carita* means "story." Carita Beach was named for the ghost stories told about the thousands who died in the eruption.

In early 1883, the Krakatoa (or Krakatau) volcano was still quiet. It was located on the small, uninhabited island of Rakata in the Dutch East Indies,[1] which was covered by tropical forests. No volcanic action had occurred there for two hundred years. In May of 1883, the volcano awoke. The earth shook and rumbled; smoke and ash poured into the air. Earthquakes continued, and volcanic activity became stronger over the next three months.

On August 26, at about 1 P.M., the first of four mighty explosions occurred. Smoke rose 27 kilometers into the air. Three more blasts, each more powerful than the last, followed the next day. The last one, at 10:02 A.M., was the most violent explosion in modern times. It was thousands of times more powerful than an atomic bomb. The walls of the volcanic cone collapsed, and seawater poured into the lava chamber below the volcano, turning 30 into superheated steam. The noise from the fourth explosion was the loudest ever heard. People heard it in Perth, Australia, 3,000 kilometers away!

4   The explosion created terrifying *tsunami*, also known as tidal waves. These towering waves, 40 meters high, crashed against 35 nearby shores. They destroyed 125 villages on both sides of the Sunda Strait and took 36,419 lives. The Sumatran town of Teluk Betung and the Javanese town of Merak completely disappeared. The waves swept over a penal settlement on Enggano Island, killing all the prisoners. In Sumatra, a wave broke a lighthouse like a 40 matchstick. In Java, a wave lifted a Dutch warship and carried it 2 kilometers up a river. The *tsunamis* sped across the Indian and Pacific oceans, and large waves hit the west coast of South America and the east coast of Africa.

5

Fig. 12.3 Krakatoa before and after eruption.

     Krakatoa's 45 explosions threw 21 cubic kilometers of ash and rock into the air. Thirty-kilogram boulders fell on islands 50 100 kilometers away. Millions of pieces of floating pumice[2] floated in the seas like rafts, blocking the path 55 of steamships. These pumice rafts washed up on beaches in Africa and South Pacific islands years later, 60 sometimes with tree roots, animal skeletons, and even human remains aboard them. The cities of Batavia (now known as Jakarta) and Singapore became as dark as night for days. The fine ash traveled around the world and spread to the northern latitudes. For years, sunrises were green and blue, and sunsets were blood red. In 65 New York and other cities, fire fighters were called out at sunset several times because people thought they saw distant fires.

6   However, colorful sunsets were not the only effect of the volcanic dust. The dust blocked the sun's heat and light, lowering the average global temperature. The year 1884 was "the year 70 without summer." Farm production in North America, Europe, and Australia dropped, and farmers suffered as their crops failed. Many had to leave their land. The weather did not return to normal until 1888.

7   Another result of the explosion was that three-quarters of the 75 island of Rakata disappeared. Only a small remnant of the old cone and two small islands remained. The rest was submerged under 80 meters of water. The remaining islands were lifeless, burned by fire and buried in ash. Therefore, they could serve as laboratories for biologists who wanted to study how life develops in a sterile 80 environment. Plant life reappeared in three years. Other than bats and birds, the first animal arrivals were spiders; using their silk like parachutes, they flew to the islands on breezes. Lizards and snakes swam, and small mammals floated there on tree branches or in coconut shells. Today the islands are full of life. 85

8   Krakatoa remained quiet until 1927, when underwater eruptions began. In 1928, a cone appeared above the waves. Russian geologist W. A. Petroeschevsky named the new volcano *Anak Krakatoa*, which means "Krakatoa's child" in Indonesian. There have been nine periods of activity since then, the most recent 90

Fig. 12.4 Anak Krakatoa erupting.

9

in 1995. The mountain grows 7 meters higher and 13 meters wider annually.

In his 2003 book *Krakatoa: The Day the World Exploded*, John Winchester writes that the Krakatoa eruption was the first great world news story. Like the waves it created, news of the event spread around the globe in days. The world was, for the first time, connected by undersea telegraph cables. Just a few years before, news from Asia had taken months to reach North America and Europe. The Krakatoa disaster showed that the world had become a much smaller place.

95

100

Notes

1. In the nineteenth century, Indonesia was colonized by the Netherlands and was known as the *Dutch East Indies*.

2. *Pumice* is a volcanic rock. It is full of air bubbles and is so lightweight that it floats.

After You Read

❯ Understanding the Reading

Answer these multiple-choice questions to see how well you understood the reading.

1. What does the author say was the most inaccurate thing about the movie *Krakatoa, East of Java*?

   (A) The name "Krakatoa" is not the real name of the volcano.
   (B) The movie suggests that the eruption took place in 1969, not in 1883.
   (C) The movie does not mention pirates and hidden treasure.
   (D) The title puts Krakatoa on the wrong side of Java.

2. Before the great eruption of 1883, Krakatoa last erupted around . . .

(A) 1403.
(B) 1683.
(C) 1803.
(D) 1881.

3. When did the greatest explosion of modern times take place?

(A) Morning, August 26, 1883
(B) Afternoon, August 26, 1883
(C) Morning, August 27, 1883
(D) Evening, August 27, 1883

4. What does the author emphasize by comparing the lighthouse to a matchstick in paragraph 4?

(A) The power of the waves
(B) The brightness of the light
(C) The age of the structure
(D) The small size of the lighthouse

5. What did the New York firefighters mentioned in paragraph 5 probably do after they were called out?

(A) They had to travel to the distant fires and put them out.
(B) They had to clean up the volcanic ash.
(C) They realized that there wasn't a fire and returned to their fire stations.
(D) They stood around and admired the colorful sunset.

6. What animals first came to the remnants of Krakatoa?

(A) Spiders
(B) Snakes and lizards
(C) Small mammals
(D) Bats and birds

7. What language did the name for the "new Krakatoa" volcano come from?

(A) Indonesian
(B) Russian
(C) English
(D) Dutch

8. How was news of the Krakatoa eruption spread so quickly?

    (A) By radio waves
    (B) By telegraph
    (C) By steamboat
    (D) By telephone

Vocabulary Building

Part 1: Fill in the blanks

Fill in the blanks in the sentences below with one of these words from the reading.

breezes	blasts	penal	terrifying	inaccurate
collapsed	matchstick	fine	uninhabited	chamber
boulder	blocked	rumbled	steam	sterile
dust	towering	remnant	submerged	rafts

1. The explorers used rubber _____ to travel down the jungle river.

2. Rock salt, which is used to melt ice on highways, is not as _____ as table salt.

3. A: Was the weather hot when you were at the beach?

    B: The temperatures were high, but it didn't feel too hot because of the cool ocean _____.

4. An espresso machine uses _____ to make coffee.

5. A large _____ rolled down the mountainside, almost crashing into a bus on the highway below.

6. In 1787, a fleet of eleven British ships brought 750 convicted criminals to Botany Bay, Australia. This _____ colony existed for sixteen years.

7. The temple was built at the foot of a _____, snow-capped mountain.

8. The first Godzilla movie was _____ for audiences.

Part 2: Matching

In the reading, there are several words that refer to a volcano erupting. Below is a picture of a volcano erupting. Match the number of the arrows with the correct part.

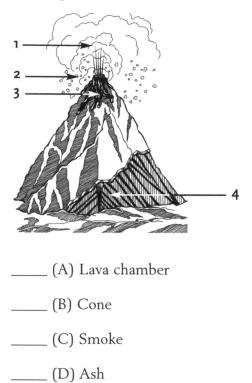

_____ (A) Lava chamber

_____ (B) Cone

_____ (C) Smoke

_____ (D) Ash

Reading Skill: Irregular Verbs

As you are reading, irregular verbs can sometimes slow you down if you are not familiar with the three key forms that they take. Even if you know the base form of a verb, you may not recognize one of the irregular forms, and these forms are not listed in all dictionaries. Of course, in order to write effectively, you will need to master irregular forms.

Verbs have three "principal parts": the base (or simple) form, the past-tense, and the past participle. The base form of a verb is the infinitive without the word *to*. This is the form of the verb that is listed in dictionaries. The past-tense and past participles of regular verbs end in *–ed*, but many verbs are irregular, and either the past-tense, the past participle, or both do not end in *–ed*.

There are only a couple of hundred irregular verbs in English, but many are among the most commonly used verbs.

Exercise: Go through the reading looking for irregular past-tense and past participle verbs (Those that do not end in –*ed.*). Find at least fifteen examples of irregular verbs (there are twenty-two in all). Then fill in the chart below. The first one is done for you.

Base form	Past tense	Past participle
1. *be*	*was*	*been*
2.		
3.		
4.		
5.		
6.		
7.		
8.		
9.		
10.		
11.		
12.		
13.		
14.		
15.		

≫ Focus on Listening

Listen to the recording of the reading "Krakatoa, West of Java." You will hear this reading two times. The first time, read along with the recording and focus on the speaker's pronunciation and intonation. The second time, listen for meaning. Do not look at the reading. Try to follow the ideas by listening only.

As you listen the second time, the speaker will stop occasionally and make statements about the reading. Decide if the statements are true or false. Fill in the space of the circled T or F according to what you hear and remember from the reading.

1. (T) (F)   5. (T) (F)

2. (T) (F)   6. (T) (F)

3. (T) (F)   7. (T) (F)

4. (T) (F)   8. (T) (F)

≫ Writing and Discussion Questions

Work with a partner or group to complete these questions.

1. The reading says that the 1969 movie about the Krakatoa eruption was inaccurate. What are some reasons why a book or a movie about an actual event might be inaccurate? Can you think of any other examples of inaccurate movies?

2. The reading tells about the eruption and "aftermath" of a terrible volcanic explosion. What effects, or "aftermath," do other disasters such as floods, typhoons, or earthquakes have?

3. "Disaster movies," which are about natural and manmade disasters are a popular type of movie. Can you think of some examples? Do you enjoy this kind of movie? Why or why not?

4. Using the Internet, get some basic information about two or three of the following volcanic eruptions. Write several sentences about each eruption that you choose.

   Mazama, U.S.A. (5000 B.C.)

   Santorini, Greece (1600 B.C.)

   Vesuvius, Italy (A.D. 79 and 1631)

   Laki, Iceland (1783)

Oshima, Japan (1783)

Unzen, Japan (1792)

Tambora, Indonesia (1815)

Nevada del Ruiz, Colombia (1845 and 1985)

Cotopaxi, Ecuador (1877)

Pelee, Martinique (1902 and 1979)

Soufriere, St. Vincent (1902)

Katmai, U.S.A. (1912)

Lamington, Papua New Guinea (1951)

Gunung Agung, Indonesia (1963)

St. Helens, U.S.A. (1979)

El Chichon, Mexico (1982)

Lake Nyos, Cameroon (1986)

Pinatubo, Phillipines (1991–1996)

4. The last line of the reading says, "The Krakatoa disaster showed that the world had become a much smaller place." What does this mean? In what ways has the world become even "smaller" since 1883?

5. Some people say that the Krakatoa eruption shows us the possible effects of air pollution on the Earth. Do you believe this is true? Why or why not?

Crossword Puzzle

Complete the puzzle with words from the reading.

Across

3 Lightweight volcanic stone

6 The sound of Krakatoa could be heard in this Australian city

8 Remainder

9 _____ Krakatoa, the "child" of Krakatoa

10 Flat boats, made of rubber or pieces of wood tied together

12 Powerful; strong

Down

1 Composed of very small particles

2 _____ Beach, or Story Beach

4 Explosions

5 Enclosed space; cavity

7 Old name for Jakarta

8 Island where the Krakatoa volcano stood

11 Gray powder produced by burning

Examination Hell

Fig. 13.1 Teacher and students at a *juku*.

Before You Read

❯ Warm-Up Questions

Discuss these questions in pairs or groups. Share your ideas with the class.

1. What is your opinion of university admissions tests? What are their advantages and disadvantages?

2. Skim the first paragraph of the reading. What is "examination hell"?

3. Have you ever taken a really difficult test? Tell the class about your experience.

≫ Vocabulary Preview

These statements come from the reading "Examination Hell." Read each statement and then answer the questions that follow. Check your answers before you begin the reading.

Every year in Japan, senior high school students face make-or-break university entrance exams. The exams are extremely difficult and the preparation period is long and grueling. That's why the testing process is called *juken jigoku,* or examination hell. For many students, these admissions exams are crucial.

1. Circle the word or phrase that means *make-or-break.*

2. There is one phrase that means *grueling.* Find and circle it.

A university degree is required for most desirable jobs, and a diploma from a leading university is almost a guarantee of career success.

3. People who have a *guarantee* of success . . .

   (A) will be successful if they work hard.
   (B) will certainly be successful.
   (C) appear to be successful, but aren't.

Students who do well in kindergarten can take admission tests to elite elementary schools, and then to choice junior and senior high schools.

4. Another word in this selection has the same meaning as *elite.* Circle it.

They say that *juku* teachers are more enthusiastic than their regular teachers and that the courses are more challenging.

5. *Enthusiastic* teachers . . .

   (A) are passionately interested in their subjects.
   (B) use the most modern methods.
   (C) are intelligent and well trained.

6. Courses that are *challenging* are . . .

   (A) almost impossible to pass.
   (B) simple and amusing.
   (C) difficult but interesting.

University days are generally carefree .

7. A *carefree* time is . . .

(A) not expensive.
(B) untroubled and relaxed.
(C) well planned.

The government also strictly regulated the cram schools.

8. If something is *regulated,* it is . . .

(A) controlled.
(B) permitted.
(C) encouraged.

The *juku* industry is no longer booming .

9. This sentence tells us that the *juku* industry is not . . .

(A) as closely regulated as it was before.
(B) in operation anymore.
(C) as successful as it once was.

Gradually , examination hell in Japan may become a thing of the past.

10. Something that happens *gradually* happens . . .

(A) easily or quickly.
(B) slowly but surely.
(C) again and again.

While You Read

Here are ten points that appear in the reading passage. There is one point for each paragraph. While you read, put the points in order from 1 to 10.

_____ The two stages of university admission tests in Japan
_____ The changing nature of examination hell in Japan
_____ Who *ronin* are
_____ Why admission tests are so important in Japan
_____ After examination hell, university heaven
_____ Why the college admission process in Japan is called "examination hell"
_____ Opinions in favor and against examination hell
_____ The early stages of examination hell
_____ Korea's former examination hell
_____ The *juku* industry

EXAMINATION HELL

1   Every year in Japan, senior high school students face make-or-break university entrance exams. The exams are extremely difficult and the preparation period is long and grueling. That's why the testing process is called *juken jigoku*, or "examination hell."

2   For many students, these admissions exams are crucial. A university degree is required for most desirable jobs, and a diploma from a leading university is almost a guarantee of career success. However, the number of applicants to the universities is far greater than the number accepted. In fact, only about one out of four students who test for leading universities are admitted the first time they test.

3   Examination hell begins early. The pressure to succeed often starts in preschool. Attending a well-known kindergarten is the first step. Students who do well in kindergarten can take admission tests to elite elementary schools, and then to choice junior and senior high schools. The pressure becomes greater as students near college age. In some ways, elementary and secondary education in Japan is one long cram session[1] for college admission.

4   Because most students in Japan are well educated, college applicants are all more or less equal. A whole industry has developed to make students more competitive. Private schools called *juku*, give students extra preparation. Often located near train stations for convenience, these "cram schools" offer courses in the evening and on weekends. Although *juku* add hours to school days, some students like them. They say that *juku* teachers are more enthusiastic than their regular teachers and that the courses are more challenging.

5   The entrance exam is actually two tests. The first, taken in January, is the Joint First Stage Achievement Test, or the Center Test. It is based on the curriculum of Japanese high schools and is a lengthy multiple-choice test. The answers to the questions appear in newspapers the following day. Several months later, students take second-stage examinations given by individual universities. Some universities use the first test to select candidates for the second-stage exam. The second-stage exams include short-answer and long essay questions, but most of the problems are again multiple choice. They cover Japanese language, mathematics, science, history, social studies, and English.

6   What about students who do not pass admission exams the first time? Many do not give up on their dreams. Instead, they become *ronin*.[2] *Ronin* often attend full-time schools called *yobiko* to study the material that is covered on the tests, take practice exams, and learn test strategies. Nearly half the students at some universities were *ronin* for a year or more.

7   For students who get through examination hell, heaven waits on the other side. University days are generally carefree. Many students join social clubs, such as jazz clubs or tennis clubs, and spend their time hanging out with friends.

8   This system of testing has both supporters and critics. Supporters say that the system is fairer than systems that depend on recommendations, essays, or high school grades. Some supporters claim that the time spent in *juku* gives Japanese students an advantage over the students of other nations and that it teaches children self-discipline. However, critics say the system creates unnecessary stress in young peoples' lives and robs them of a happy childhood. This leads to depression and exhaustion. There is a saying among high school students: "pass with four, fail with five."

In other words, students who sleep five hours a night will fail. Critics also say that, because the exams test memorization of facts, students do not learn analysis and creativity. 60

9   In the recent past, Japan's neighbor Korea also had examination hell (*sih m chiok* in Korean). Like Japanese, Koreans attended after-school cram schools (*hogwan*) to prepare for the tests. However, about fifteen years ago, the Korean government forced universities to accept more students, and the admission process became less 65 competitive. The government also strictly regulated the cram schools. College admission tests in Korea are still difficult, but not nearly as hard as they were in the 1980s.

10   Something similar seems to be happening in Japan. Students say that the tests have become slightly less demanding in recent years. 70 Also, the government has encouraged universities to consider other standards besides test scores. The *juku* industry is no longer booming. Meanwhile, Japan's population is aging. Every year, fewer people of college age compete for space in universities. Gradually, examination hell in Japan may become a thing of the past. 75

Notes

1. During a *cram session*, students study a lot of material in a very brief time, usually to prepare for a test. The verb *cram* means to pack many things into a small space (to cram clothes into a suitcase).

2. In medieval Japan, *ronin* were traveling samurai (warriors) without masters. Students in Japan who must repeat the admission exams are called *ronin* because neither the high school nor the university is their "master."

After You Read

❯ Understanding the Reading

Answer these multiple-choice questions to see how well you understood the reading.

1. What percentage of students who test for top universities in Japan are admitted the first time they test?

   (A) 1%
   (B) 4%
   (C) 25%
   (D) 75%

2. When is the pressure of examination hell strongest in Japan?

   (A) In preschool and kindergarten
   (B) In junior high school
   (C) In senior high school
   (D) At the university

3. Some students enjoy studying at a *juku* because . . .

   (A) the classes are easy to pass.
   (B) they are taught by teachers from their regular schools.
   (C) they replace regular classes on weekdays.
   (D) the teachers and the material are exciting.

4. These are four proverbs (old sayings) commonly used in English. Which best suits *ronin* who are studying at a *yobiko*?

   (A) "Two heads are better than one."
   (B) "If at first you don't succeed, try, try again."
   (C) "The more things change, the more they stay the same."
   (D) "The taller they are, the harder they fall."

5. A critic of the current examination system in Japan might say which of the following?

   (A) Recommendations are not a fair way to judge university applicants.
   (B) The *juku* system teaches Japanese students to discipline themselves.
   (C) Preparing for difficult tests gives Japanese students an advantage over students from other countries.
   (D) The testing system emphasizes only memorization, not analysis or creativity.

6. What do Japanese students mean when they say "pass with four, fail with five"?

   (A) If you sleep only four hours a night you will succeed on the test, but not if you sleep five hours a night.
   (B) If you study four hours a night, you will do better than if you study five hours a night.
   (C) At the university, you should take four classes, not five.
   (D) You can study in a group with four other students, but not with more than four.

7. What was one step the Korean government took to solve the problem of examination hell?

(A) To open special schools to help students prepare for tests
(B) To make universities accept more students
(C) To change the test from multiple-choice to essay
(D) To reduce the number of questions on the test

8. What is one reason examination hell may be ending in Japan?
(A) The government has started to eliminate cram schools.
(B) More students from Japan are applying to universities in other countries.
(C) There are fewer people of college age in Japan.
(D) There is now only one admission test, not two.

➤ Vocabulary Building

Fill in the blanks in the sentences below with one of these words or phrases from the reading.

make-or-break	elite	hanging out	grueling	enthusiastic
memorization	guarantee	essay	leading	convenience
a thing of the past	gradually	admitted	carefree	curriculum

1. My father says he was always studying when he was in school, but my uncle says that he spent his time _____ with his friends.

2. Mr. Jackson was a _____ candidate for mayor until his financial problems were discovered.

3. I don't like multiple-choice tests. I prefer _____ exams so that I can explain my ideas.

4. Katie was a very _____ person in high school, but when she went to medical school, she became very serious and hardworking.

5. The triathlon race is a very _____ sports event that includes running, swimming, and bicycling for long distances.

6. In my country, _____ students mainly attend private high schools.

7. Doctors hope to develop a vaccine against malaria. Soon, they hope, that disease will be _____.

8. If Olga does a good job on this project, she will be promoted, but if she doesn't, she'll be fired. This is really a _____ assignment for her.

Reading Skill: Making Inferences

Ideas and information in a reading are not always given directly. Sometimes they are *implied*. To understand the author's ideas, the reader makes an *inference*. Another expression for making inferences is *reading between the lines*. This can be a difficult skill to master, but it is an important one. By practicing this skill, you will become a better reader.

Example: Read this sentence taken from the reading:

Often located near train stations for convenience, these "cram schools" offer courses in the evening and on weekends.

What is directly stated? The schools are near trains for students' convenience.

What can be inferred?

1. Many students take the train to go to cram schools.

2. Many students take the train to go to cram schools on weekends.

3. If cram schools were not located near train stations, fewer students would attend.

Exercise: Following are sentences and short paragraphs related to the reading. Read each sentence and the sentence that follows. If the sentence that follows is a valid inference based on the first sentence, mark it **I**. If not, mark it **X**.

In Japan, graduation from a good university used to mean employment at a good company for a lifetime.

_____ 1. Today, graduates from a good Japanese university are assured that they will have lifelong employment with the best companies.

Students can take entrance examinations at more than one university. Many high school seniors and *ronin* travel all over Japan to take examinations at the schools of their choice.

_____ 2. University entrance exams in Japan are not given on the same day.

English, like most exam subjects, is taught primarily so that the students can pass the entrance exam. Therefore, while students generally develop a strong vocabulary they often cannot communicate fluently.

_____   3. Questions in the English-language section of entrance exams primarily test vocabulary more than communication skills.

The government asks commuters to arrive at work one hour later than usual on the day of the college entrance exams in Korea to avoid making the test-takers late. If students do have trouble getting to the place of their tests, emergency vehicles are waiting to help them get there in time. During the language dictation sections, buses, trains, and taxis must slow down near the exam sites, and use of horns is prohibited.

_____   4. The Korean government is interested in making sure the testing situation is fair and convenient for all students.

In the last few weeks before the test, mothers, fathers, and siblings walk quietly around the house so that they do not disturb the students' concentration. Mothers read magazines to get recipes for foods that will increase the students' alertness. Some mothers even take courses to learn about the test and how to help their students get the highest possible grade. After the test, family members wait in agony to learn the results of the test.

_____   5. Mothers and other family members go through their own "examination hell."

Magazine and newspaper articles sometimes give the impression that all Japanese students experience examination hell. In fact, only about half of all high school students attend *juku* and not all of them concentrate on test preparation. Not even all those who take test preparation courses feel intense pressure to do well on the exams.

_____   6. Newspapers and magazines present an accurate picture of examination hell.

➤ Focus on Listening

Listen to the recording of the reading "Examination Hell." You will hear this reading two times. The first time, read along with the recording and focus on the speaker's pronunciation and intonation. The second time, listen for meaning. Do not look at the reading. Try to follow the ideas by listening only.

As you listen the second time, the speaker will stop occasionally and make statements about the reading. Decide if the statements are true or false. Fill in the space of the circled T or F according to what you hear and remember from the reading.

1. Ⓣ Ⓕ   5. Ⓣ Ⓕ
2. Ⓣ Ⓕ   6. Ⓣ Ⓕ
3. Ⓣ Ⓕ   7. Ⓣ Ⓕ
4. Ⓣ Ⓕ   8. Ⓣ Ⓕ

➤ Writing and Discussion Questions

Work with a partner or group to complete these questions.

1. Tell a partner your experiences in applying to colleges or universities (or what you think this experience will be like). Then take notes as your partner tells you of his or her experiences. Tell the class what you learned about your partner's experiences.

2. Visit the Internet site of one university in another country and find out their basic requirements for admission for international students. Summarize what you learn in one paragraph.

3. Imagine that you are changing the standards for admission at your university. Decide the importance of each standard. Score each from 1 to 100, with 100 the best score. Give reasons for your choice.

_____ letters of recommendation   _____ student-written essays

_____ university-designed admissions tests   _____ interviews with admissions officers

_____ standardized admissions tests   _____ high-school grades

What other possible standards can you think of?

» Crossword Puzzle

Complete the puzzle with words from the reading.

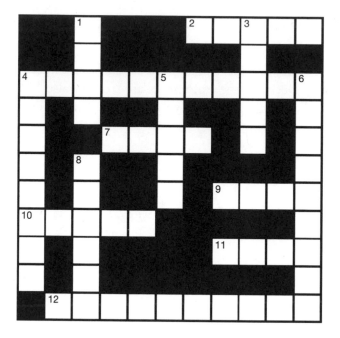

Across

2 Make-or- _____
4 Difficult but interesting
7 A thing of the _____
9 Japanese cram school
10 A student who fails to get admitted to a university in Japan on his or her first attempt
11 Pass with four, _____ with five.
12 The ability to think of new ideas

Down

1 To study a lot of material in a limited time
3 Top; select; choice
4 Without worries; no problems
5 A long piece of writing
6 Slowly; step by step
8 The first stage of the admissions test in Japan is sometimes called the _____ test.

The Mummy's Curse

Fig. 14.1

Before You Read

» Warm-Up Questions

Discuss these questions in pairs or groups. Share your ideas with the class.

1. What is a mummy? What do you know about Egyptian mummies? How did you find out about them?

2. Who is King Tut? Skim the first paragraph of the reading. What do you learn about him from that paragraph?

3. Look at the photograph on this page. What do you think is happening?

❱ Vocabulary Preview

These statements come from the reading "The Mummy's Curse." Read each statement and then answer the questions that follow. Check your answers before you begin the reading.

Tut's body was mummified and placed in a tomb with everything a person might need in the afterlife: jewelry, gold coins, clothing, food. These treasures , of course, attracted tomb robbers.

1. Underline some examples of *treasures* given in the selection above.

They built false doors and secret rooms and sealed the tombs with rock. Then they put curses on anyone who tried to enter.

2. Tombs that are *sealed* with rock . . .

    (A) are built out of rock.
    (B) are difficult to enter.
    (C) are tombs that can be opened by using rocks.

Since the snake was a symbol of the Pharaohs, Reis believed this was bad luck, and he urged Carter not to enter the tomb.

3. In other words, Reis . . . go into the tomb.

    (A) strongly advised Carter not to
    (B) ordered Carter not to
    (C) refused to help Carter

The tomb was full of treasures that would stun the world.

4. To *stun* is to . . .

    (A) alarm.
    (B) surprise.
    (C) delight.

Later it was discovered that King Tut had a wound in the same place on his cheek as Carnarvon.

5. A *wound* is . . .

    (A) an injury.
    (B) a painted symbol.
    (C) a piece of jewelry.

And back in England, Carnarvon's three-legged dog Susie began to howl and then died suddenly.

6. When a dog *howls*, it . . .

   (A) bites someone.
   (B) barks.
   (C) makes a loud, sad sound.

However, within ten years, journalists reported that over twelve people connected with the discovery of the tomb had died in suspicious ways.

7. When people die in *suspicious* ways, . . .

   (A) they die in violent ways.
   (B) their methods of death are strange and mysterious.
   (C) they die very suddenly.

"Death will come on swift wings to those who disturb the Pharaoh's rest," the curse supposedly said.

8. Another word for *swift* is . . .

   (A) silent.
   (B) long.
   (C) fast.

In 2002, Mark Nelson, an Australian medical researcher at Monash University, investigated the curse. He studied the lifespan of all the Europeans present at the opening of the tomb and the discovery of the mummy. He also researched the lifespan of other westerners living in Egypt at the time.

9. There are two words close in meaning to *investigated*. Circle them.

Dr. Nelson said, "I found no evidence for the curse's existence. . . . Perhaps finally, like the tragic boy king Tutankhamen, the curse may now be put to rest."

10. *Tragic* means . . .

   (A) sad and unfortunate.
   (B) little known.
   (C) wealthy and wonderful.

While You Read

Here are eight points that appear in the reading passage. There is one point for each paragraph. While you read, put the points in order from 1 to 8.

_____ A scientific study of the curse
_____ Introducing the boy king
_____ The opening of the tomb
_____ Carter and the canary
_____ What Carter might have thought of the study
_____ Mummies and tombs
_____ The Death of Lord Carnarvon
_____ The story of Tut's curse

THE MUMMY'S CURSE

1   He is called the "boy king." He became pharaoh[1] at age nine. He   1
died at nineteen, probably murdered by his own general, Horemheb,
who later became pharaoh. Although we know little about his life,
Tutankhamen, or King Tut, is, the most famous Egyptian king. He
died 3,300 years ago, but some believe his curse[2] still has power.   5

2   The curse became famous some eighty years ago, when King
Tut's tomb was discovered. Like other important Egyptians, Tut's
body was mummified[3] and placed in a tomb with everything a
person might need in the afterlife:[4] jewelry, gold coins, clothing,
food. These treasures, of course, attracted tomb robbers. Egyptian   10
tomb builders tried to protect the tombs from intruders. They built
these burial chambers in secret places such as the Valley of Kings.[5]
They built false doors and secret rooms and sealed the tombs with
rock. Then they put curses on anyone who tried to enter.

3   However, not even curses stopped the tomb robbers. Almost all of   15
the tombs were robbed in ancient or medieval times. By the time
young British archaeologist Howard Carter arrived in Egypt in 1891,

Fig. 14.2 Carnarvon and Howard entering the tomb.

most ancient tombs had been broken into. Carter came to Egypt with the dream of finding one undisturbed tomb. He searched for years without luck and ran out of money. Then, in 1918, Carter met Lord Carnarvon, a British aristocrat, who gave him the money he needed to continue. Five years later, Carter returned to England to meet with Carnarvon. While in England, Carter bought a canary[6] and took it back to Egypt. His Egyptian foreman, Reis Ahmed, believed this "golden bird" was a good sign. "It will lead us to the tomb," he said. A week later, Carter found the hidden steps leading to King Tut's tomb. But that night, a snake entered Carter's house and killed the canary. Since the snake was a symbol of the pharaohs, Reis believed this was bad luck, and he urged Carter not to enter the tomb.

4 Carter, of course, didn't listen to the foreman's warning. He waited anxiously for Carnarvon to come from England for the opening of the tomb. On November 26, 1923, the tomb was unsealed, Carter looked in with his flashlight. "Do you see anything?" Carnarvon asked. "Yes, wonderful things." Carter found a golden sarcophagus.[7] Inside the sarcophagus was the mummy of the boy king in a golden mask. The tomb was full of treasures that would stun the world. It was a time of triumph for Carter and Carnarvon.

Fig. 14.3 King Tut's funerary mask.

5   Carnarvon was unable to celebrate for long, however. A week   50
after the discovery, he was bitten on the cheek by a mosquito.
When he was shaving, he cut open the mosquito bite and it became
infected. Within a week, he was dead. Later, it was discovered that
King Tut had a wound in the same place on his cheek as Carnarvon.
Moreover, at the moment Carnarvon died, Cairo's electricity went   55
out. And back in England, Carnarvon's three-legged dog Susie
began to howl and then died suddenly.

6   According to newspapers, Carnarvon was the first victim of the
"curse of King Tut." Reporters claimed that Carter had found a
tablet with the curse inscribed on it and hidden it so that his   60
workers would not be afraid. Carter himself always denied that
this was true. However, within ten years, journalists reported that
over twelve people connected with the discovery of the tomb had
died in suspicious ways. As late as the 1970s, when a guard at the
King Tut exhibition in San Francisco had a heart attack, people   65
blamed the curse.

7   "Death will come on swift wings to those who disturb the
Pharaoh's rest," the curse supposedly said. Was this true? In 2002,
Mark Nelson, an Australian medical researcher at Monash
University, investigated the curse. He studied the lifespan of all the   70
Europeans present at the opening of the tomb and the discovery of
the mummy. He also researched the lifespan of other westerners
living in Egypt at the time. Dr. Nelson said, "I found no evidence for
the curse's existence. . . . Perhaps finally, like the tragic boy king
Tutankhamen, the curse may now be put to rest."   75

8   Tut's discoverer Howard Carter would have been pleased with
Nelson's study. "All sane people should dismiss such stories with
contempt," Carter once said. Carter, by the way, lived to be sixty-six.

Notes

1. The *pharaohs* were the rulers of ancient Egypt.

2. A *curse* is a set of words that are spoken or written to protect someone or something. Some people believe that curses have the power to cause harm to others.

3. Wealthy and powerful Egyptians were *mummified* after death. Their bodies were cleaned and treated with chemicals and herbs to kill bacteria and then dried out with salt. Finally, they were wrapped in strips of cotton.

4. A belief in the *afterlife*, or life after death, is common to many religions, including that of the ancient Egyptians.

5. *The Valley of Kings* was a desolate area near Luxor, Egypt. It was used as a burial place for pharaohs because it was in a remote area and did not seem a likely place for kings to be buried.

6. A *canary* is a small yellow bird often kept as a pet.

7. A *sarcophagus* is a box used to hold human remains.

After You Read

≫ Understanding the Reading

Answer these multiple-choice questions to see how well you understood the reading

1. Tutankhamen was pharaoh for . . .

   (A) one year.
   (B) ten years.
   (C) nineteen years.
   (D) eighty years.

2. Why was it difficult for scientists to find tombs with treasures?

   (A) Because they were buried deep under the desert
   (B) Because the builders hid the tombs so carefully
   (C) Because tomb robbers had already broken in and stolen the treasures
   (D) Because they had false doors and secret rooms sealed with rock

3. Carter returned to England to meet with Lord Carnarvon in . . .

   (A) 1891.
   (B) 1896.
   (C) 1918.
   (D) 1923.

4. What did Carter's foreman Reis Ahmed first think of the canary?

   (A) That it would bring good luck
   (B) That it was a symbol of the pharaohs
   (C) That it was a sign of bad luck
   (D) That it could be used to find the tomb

5. Which of these facts about Lord Carnarvon's dog is NOT revealed in the reading?

   (A) Her name
   (B) What country she lived in at the time she died
   (C) How many legs she had
   (D) What the exact cause of her death was

6. Who promoted the idea of King Tut's curse?

   (A) Howard Carter
   (B) Lord Carnarvon
   (C) Journalists
   (D) Mark Nelson

7. According to journalists, who was the most recent victim of King Tut's curse?

   (A) Lord Carnarvon
   (B) Susie, Lord Carnarvon's dog
   (C) Howard Carter
   (D) A museum guard in San Francisco

8. Mark Nelson's research was mainly about the . . .

   (A) lifespan of westerners in Carter's party and other westerners in Egypt.
   (B) lifespan of the ancient pharaohs.
   (C) deaths of Lord Carnarvon and Howard Carter.
   (D) location of tombs in the Valley of Kings.

❯ Vocabulary Building

Fill in the blanks in the sentences below with one of these words or phrases from the reading.

broken into	anxiously	howl	swift	undisturbed
stun	victim	supposedly	lifespan	foreman
triumph	inscribed	symbol	infected	suspicious
put to rest	sealed	urged	wound	blamed

1. People in Okinawa have a longer _____ than people anywhere else in the world. Scientists have studied Okinawans to try to learn why they live so long.

2. My boss _____ me for the mistake, but I had nothing to do with it.

3. The museum was _____ by daring art thieves who stole some priceless paintings.

4. The _____ Ø is sometimes used in place of the symbol 0 to mean zero.

5. During the storm, we could hear the wind _____ outside the cabin.

6. The government _____ up the old abandoned mine so that no one would get hurt in it.

7. The name of the company was _____ in stone over the doorway of the corporate headquarters.

8. Marcella washed her cut with antibacterial soap so that it wouldn't become _____.

Reading Skill: Understanding Prefixes

A prefix is a group of letters that comes before the base form of a word. A prefix changes the meaning of words. (A suffix—a group of letters at the *end* of a word—changes the way a word is used.)

Knowing the meaning of common prefixes helps you in two important ways. First, it helps you build your vocabulary and quickly guess the meaning of unknown words in a reading, especially if you are familiar with the root. Second, knowing how prefixes are used with words can also make your writing clearer and more precise.

Here is a list of some of the prefixes used on words in readings in this book:

Prefix	Meaning	Example
dis-	not	disagreed
inter-	between	intercontinental
co-, com-, con-	together	coexist, composed, connect
in-	not	independent
over-	too much	overrated
un-	not	unexpected
re-	again	reaction
pre-	before	prehistoric
mon- or mono-	one	monopoly
extra-	beyond	extraordinary
il-	not	illiterate
non-	not	nonrefundable
multi-	many	multinational
sub-	under	submerged

Exercise: Match the words on the left with the definitions on the right.

_____ 1. monarchy   (A) having more than one use

_____ 2. confluence   (B) place where two rivers flow together

_____ 3. predict	(C) confused; not orderly
_____ 4. nonsense	(D) rule by one person
_____ 5. overprotective	(E) put one thing between others
_____ 6. inattentive	(F) not to the point; not related
_____ 7. multipurpose	(G) working together
_____ 8. disorganized	(H) something that is not logical
_____ 9. intersperse	(I) being too cautious or careful
_____ 10. cooperative	(J) not watching or listening
_____ 11. irrelevant	(K) against the law
_____ 12. illegal	(L) tell someone that everything is all right
_____ 13. reassure	(M) break into pieces; fall apart
_____ 14. disintegrate	(N) to say what will happen before it happens

» Focus on Listening

Listen to the recording of the reading "The Mummy's Curse." You will hear this reading two times. The first time, read along with the recording and focus on the speaker's pronunciation and intonation. The second time, listen for meaning. Do not look at the reading. Try to follow the ideas by listening only.

As you listen the second time, the speaker will stop occasionally and make statements about the reading. Decide if the statements are true or false. Fill in the space of the circled T or F according to what you hear and remember from the reading.

1. (T) (F)   5. (T) (F)

2. (T) (F)   6. (T) (F)

3. (T) (F)   7. (T) (F)

4. (T) (F)   8. (T) (F)

≫ Writing and Discussion Questions

Work with a partner or group to complete these questions.

1. People who believe in curses are usually considered *superstitious*. What does *superstitious* mean? Discuss some common superstitions and your opinions of them.

2. In addition to King Tut, there are other famous Egyptian mummies. Using the Internet for research, report to the class on one of these mummies. Illustrate your report with photos from the Internet if possible.

    Seti I   Amenhotep III   Ramses II   Thutmose IV   Nefertiti

≫ Crossword Puzzle

Complete the puzzle with words from the reading.

Across

1 Preserved and prepared for the afterlife
2 A container for mummies
7 A covering for the face
8 Mentally healthy
10 Yellow bird
11 To surprise or shock

Down

1 Blood-sucking insect
3 Lord _____, Carter's financial backer
4 Make a sudden, sorrowful sound
5 Symbol of the pharaoh
6 Ancient Egyptian king
9 Tutankhamen's nickname

Vocabulary Index

Reading Skills Chart

Reading Skill	Unit Section	Page Number
Chronological Order	Reading Skill	73
Comprehension (general)	Understanding the Reading	7, 20, 32, 46, 58, 71, 83, 95, 108, 120, 132, 145, 158, 171
Conditional Sentences	Reading Skill	123
Inferences	Reading Skill	161
Paraphrasing	Reading Skill	135
Passive Sentences	Reading Skill	60

Patterns of Organization
  analysis
  cause
  classification
  comparison
  contrast
  definition
  description
  effect
  examples
  narration
  persuasion
  problem/solution
    (question/answer)
  process
	Reading Skill	98

Reading Skill	Unit Section	Page Number
Predicting • from illustrations	Warm-Up Questions	1, 14, 27, 40, 52, 64, 89, 103, 114, 127, 139, 165
• from title	Warm-Up Questions	1, 41, 103, 139
Prefixes	Reading Skill	174
Previewing	Warm-Up Questions	1, 14, 27, 40, 52, 64, 77, 89, 103, 114, 127, 139, 153, 165
	Vocabulary Preview	2, 15, 28, 41, 53, 65, 78, 90, 104, 115, 128, 140, 154, 166
Reading for Main Ideas	While You Read	4, 17, 29, 43, 54, 66, 80, 91, 106, 117, 130, 141, 155, 168
Scanning	Reading Skill Warm-Up Questions	111 77, 114, 127
Skimming	Reading Skill Warm-Up Questions	48 64, 103, 139, 153, 165
Suffixes (in Word Forms, below)	Reading Skill	23, 35
Verbs, Irregular	Reading Skill	148
Vocabulary • definitions	Vocabulary Preview	2, 15, 28, 41, 53, 65, 78, 90, 104, 115, 128, 140, 154, 166
	Vocabulary Building	8, 22, 34, 47, 59, 72, 84, 97, 110, 122, 134, 147, 160, 173
	Crossword	13, 26, 39, 51, 63, 76, 88, 102, 113, 126, 138, 152, 164, 176

Reading Skill	Unit Section	Page Number
• from context	Vocabulary Preview	2, 15, 28, 41, 53, 65, 78, 90, 104, 115, 128, 140, 154, 166
	Vocabulary Building	8, 22, 34, 47, 59, 72, 84, 97, 110, 122, 134, 147, 160, 173
• synonyms (working with)	Reading Skill	85, 111, 135
• special terms (topic-specific, jargon)	Notes	7, 20, 32, 45, 57, 70, 83, 95, 108, 120, 132, 145, 158, 171
Vocabulary from Context		
General Meaning	Reading Skill	85
Right/Specific Meaning	Reading Skill	9
Word Forms		
Nouns, Verbs, Adj., Adv.	Reading Skill	23
Personal Nouns and Terms of Origin	Reading Skill	35